American
English in Mind

Herbert Puchta & Jeff Stranks

Student's Book **1**

CAMBRIDGE
UNIVERSITY PRESS

CAMBRIDGE
UNIVERSITY PRESS

University Printing House, Cambridge CB2 8BS, United Kingdom

One Liberty Plaza, 20th Floor, New York, NY 10006, USA

477 Williamstown Road, Port Melbourne, VIC 3207, Australia

4843/24, 2nd Floor, Ansari Road, Daryaganj, Delhi – 110002, India

79 Anson Road, #06–04/06, Singapore 079906

Cambridge University Press is part of the University of Cambridge.

It furthers the University's mission by disseminating knowledge in the pursuit of education, learning and research at the highest international levels of excellence.

www.cambridge.org
Information on this title: www.cambridge.org/9780521733335

First published 2011
20 19 18 17 16 15

Printed in the United Kingdom by Latimer Trend

A catalogue record for this publication is available from the British Library

Library of Congress Cataloging-in-Publication Data

Puchta, Herbert.
American English in mind. 1 / Herbert Puchta & Jeff Stranks.
p. cm.

ISBN 978-0-521-73333-5 (Student bk. 1) – ISBN 978-0-521-73334-2 (Combo 1A) – ISBN 978-0-521-73335-9 (Combo 1B) – ISBN 978-0-521-73339-7 (Workbook 1) – ISBN 978-0-521-73340-3 (Teacher's ed.1) – ISBN 978-0-521-73341-0 (Class Audio 1) – ISBN 978-0-521-73327-4 (Classware 1) – ISBN 978-0-521-73342-7 (Testmaker 1)

1. English language–Textbooks for foreign speakers. 2. English language–Spoken English–Problems, exercises, etc. 3. English language–Grammar–Problems, exercises, etc. 4. Vocabulary–Problems, exercises, etc. 5. English language–United States. 6. Americanisms.
I. Stranks, Jeff . II. Title.

PE1128.P833 2010

428.2'4076–dc22

ISBN 978-0-521-73333-5 Student's Book 1
ISBN 978-0-521-73334-2 Combo 1A
ISBN 978-0-521-73335-9 Combo 1B
ISBN 978-0-521-73339-7 Workbook 1
ISBN 978-0-521-73340-3 Teacher's Edition 1
ISBN 978-0-521-73341-0 Class Audio 1
ISBN 978-0-521-73327-4 Classware 1
ISBN 978-0-521-73342-7 Testmaker 1

Art direction, book design and layout: Pentacor plc
Photo research: Pronk and Associates

Contents

Unit	Grammar	Vocabulary	Pronunciation
1 Welcome	Possessive adjectives *have* *there is / there are* Prepositions of place	Greetings and introductions, colors, rooms and furniture	/h/ (*have*)
2 Some of the rules	Imperatives Adverbs of frequency Object pronouns *can/can't* for ability *there is / there are* (negative and questions) + *a/an/any*	Activity verbs, places, time, clothes, money and prices Everyday English	*can/can't*
CHECK YOUR PROGRESS			
3 Free time	Simple present (affirmative and negative; questions and short answers) *like + ing*	Hobbies and interests, school subjects	/n/ (ma<u>n</u>) and /ŋ/ (so<u>ng</u>)
4 Helping other people	Present continuous for activities happening now Simple present vs. present continuous	Housework Everyday English	/ər/ (w<u>or</u>ld)
CHECK YOUR PROGRESS			
5 Who's your hero?	Simple past; *be* and regular verbs (affirmative and negative); *was born / were born*	Multi-word verbs (1) Memory words	*was* and *were* *-ed* endings
6 Making friends	Simple past (regular and irregular verbs; questions and short answers)	Time expressions (past), sports Everyday English	Word stress
CHECK YOUR PROGRESS			
7 Successful people	*have to / don't have to*	Jobs, work and money	*have to*
8 Eat for life.	Count and noncount nouns *a/an, some* and *any, much* and *many*	Food and drink Everyday English	/ə/ (th<u>e</u>)
CHECK YOUR PROGRESS			
9 Learning languages	Comparatives and superlatives	Language learning	*than*
10 We're going on vacation.	Present continuous for future arrangements	Future time expressions, vacation activities Everyday English	/θ/ (<u>th</u>ink) and /ð/ (<u>th</u>at)
CHECK YOUR PROGRESS			
11 It'll never happen.	*will/won't*	Expressions to talk about the future, expressions to talk about future technology	*'ll*
12 Don't give up.	*too* + adjective, adverbs	The weather Everyday English	/oʊ/ (g<u>o</u>)
CHECK YOUR PROGRESS			
13 Promises, promises	*be going to* (intentions and predictions), *must/can't*	Multi-word verbs (2), prepositions	*be going to*
14 What a brave person!	First conditional, *when* and *if*	Adjectives of feeling Everyday English	Stress in conditional sentences
CHECK YOUR PROGRESS			
15 Travelers' tales	*should/shouldn't, What's it like?*	Personality adjectives, adjectives for expressing opinions	Silent consonants
16 Crazy records	Present perfect + *ever/never*	Verbs and noun pairs, expressions about sleep Everyday English	*have* and *has* in the present perfect
CHECK YOUR PROGRESS			

Pages 114–122 Pronunciation • Speaking exercises • Projects • Irregular verbs

Speaking & Functions	Listening	Reading	Writing
Greeting and introducing people Talking about your: family and friends; home and furniture Describing your dream house	Talking about family	Web page: My friends Culture in mind: More than a place to sleep	Description of your dream house
Talking about: how often you do an activity; what you can and can't do Describing: your city or town; clothes Asking about prices of clothes Last but not least: planning a business	*Can* and *can't* dialogue	Rules brochure: Westside Pool Photostory: Too much homework	Email about a club and its rules
Talking about school subjects and hobbies Expressing likes and dislikes Interviewing / being interviewed	An interview about a hobby	Article: An unusual hobby Culture in mind: School life	Email about hobbies and interests
Talking about: activities happening now; housework Last but not least: arranging to meet and making plans	Radio interview with a volunteer in Namibia, Africa	Article: Helping at a hospital Photostory: Let's help him out.	Email about preparing for a party
Talking about: the past; when/where you were born Giving a presentation on your hero	Presentation of "my hero"	Article: Erin Brockovich Culture in mind: Remembering heroes	Description of your hero
Asking about the past Last but not least: the alibi game	Television story Song: "You've Got a Friend in Me"	Article: The friendship that changed the world Photostory: Not a nice thing to say	Diary entry or email about a fun weekend
Talking about obligations Describing job requirements Talking about a job you want to do when you finish school	Talking about success Description on future jobs	Article: What does "success" mean? Article: Racing to success Culture in mind: Teenagers earning money	Description of a job
Talking about food and staying fit Ordering food in a cafeteria Last but not least: talking about food and places to eat	School cafeteria dialogue	Article: A long and healthy life Photostory: Two scoops of ice cream	Paragraph about food and staying fit
Comparing things Talking about learning English	Descriptions and interview about language learning An interview with David Crystal	Article: Speaking in many tongues Culture in mind: Teen talk	Description or email about language learning
Talking about future plans Discussing vacation plans Last but not least: talking about vacations	Radio show about family vacations Dialogue about vacation plans	Magazine: Family vacations can be fun! Travel brochure: Welcome to Cape Town – the city that has everything! Photostory: Having fun?	Email about a trip
Making predictions Talking about your future life Inventing a new technology for the future	Future predictions Song: "When I'm Sixty-four"	Article: Getting the future wrong! Culture in mind: The future of technology	Text predicting the future
Describing actions Relating Hermann Maier's life story Last but not least: talking about famous sportspeople	Dialogue about the life of Hermann Maier	Article: Jungle survival Photostory: Keep running.	Email giving advice to a friend
Talking about intentions Talking about a song	Dialogue about a New Year's resolutions Song: "Wonderful World, Beautiful People"	Article: Celebrate New Year's Eve Culture in mind: Reggae music	Email about your New Year's Eve
Expressing future possibilities Talking about how brave a person is Last but not least: talking about situations where you are brave / not brave	Dialogues about bravery	Article: Subway hero Photostory: Chicken	A movie, book or TV show review
Giving advice and recommendations Talking about what somebody is like	Dialogue about different customs around the world A quiz about U.S. culture	Quiz: What do you know about U.S. culture? Culture in mind: Heroic Ulises on a journey of hope	Email giving tips to a tourist
Talking about life experiences; when you do everyday activities Last but not least: talking about things you've done / never done	Conversation about a strange world record	Article: You've never seen anything like this! Article: He holds the records – for records! Photostory: What's next?	Email about a visit to Los Angeles

1 Welcome

* Grammar: possessive adjectives; the verb *have*; *there is / there are*; prepositions of place
* Vocabulary: greetings and introductions; colors, rooms and furniture

1 Read and listen

* Greetings and introductions

a Look at the pictures. What are these people doing? Read the dialogue quickly to check your ideas.

b ▶ **CD1 T02** Now read the dialogue again and listen. Then practice the dialogue in groups of three.

Liz: Hi! My name is Liz.

Jack: Hello, Liz. I'm Jack.

Liz: Nice to meet you. Oh, hi, Monica. How are you?

Monica: I'm fine, thanks. How about you?

Liz: I'm OK, thanks. Jack, this is my friend, Monica.

Jack: Nice to meet you.

c Look at the pictures of Jack's friends on his web page. Where are they from? Read the text quickly to check your ideas.

My friends

Hi, my name is Jack. I'm from the United States. Welcome to my page!

This is my new friend Monica. I'm glad we are friends. She's from Italy. Her family is in Rome. She lives here now. She's here for one year. She chats with her family online all the time!

This is my friend Carlos. He's really cool. He's from Guatemala. His family is big – three brothers and one sister! Their house is in the country. Guatemala is a great place for an adventure vacation. There are volcanoes, beaches, jungles and Mayan ruins. I want to visit him someday.

These two friends are Barbara and Ken. Barbara and Ken are from Canada, but their parents are from different places. Ken's parents are from India. Barbara's parents are from Poland. They go to same school. They live in the same building in Toronto.

My online friends are all really great. We want to get together and have a party someday ...but in which country?

d ▶ **CD1 T03** Now read the text again and listen. Mark the statements *T* (true) or *F* (false).

1 Monica is in Rome now. ☐

2 Carlos's house is in the country. ☐

3 Ken isn't from India. ☐

4 Carlos and Barbara go to the same school. ☐

Grammar review

✳ Possessive adjectives

Read the message from Liz's e-pal, Yolanda. Complete the sentences with *my, your, his, her, our* or *their*.

LOOK!

America	American
Canada	Canadian
China	Chinese
Colombia	Colombian
Guatemala	Guatemalan
India	Indian
Japan	Japanese
Poland	Polish

from: yolandamendez@aeim.cup

subject: Hello!

Hi, Liz!

Thanks for the email! I like the photos of ¹ ___your___ friends and family. ² _____ mom and dad look really nice in the photo. What are ³ _____ names?

Now I'll tell you about me and ⁴ _____ family here in Colombia. I have two brothers. ⁵ _____ names are Gabriel and Eduardo, and they're 18 and 19. My mother is American, and ⁶ _____ name is Christine. Dad is Colombian. He's from Cali, and ⁷ _____ name is Luis. We live in Bogotá. ⁸ _____ house has four bedrooms and a small yard. We have a dog, and we think he's really great. ⁹ _____ name is Zak.

Please write again soon!

Your friend,

Yolanda

✳ The verb *have*

a ▶ **CD1 T04** Listen to the dialogue between Jeff and Monica and answer the questions.

1 How many brothers and sisters does Jeff have?

2 How many brothers and sisters does Monica have?

b ▶ **CD1 T04** Listen again and complete the table.

	Age	Hair color	Eye color
Paul			
Debra			
Lisa			

c Follow the lines and say the sentences with *have/has* and *doesn't have*.

My brother doesn't have a computer.

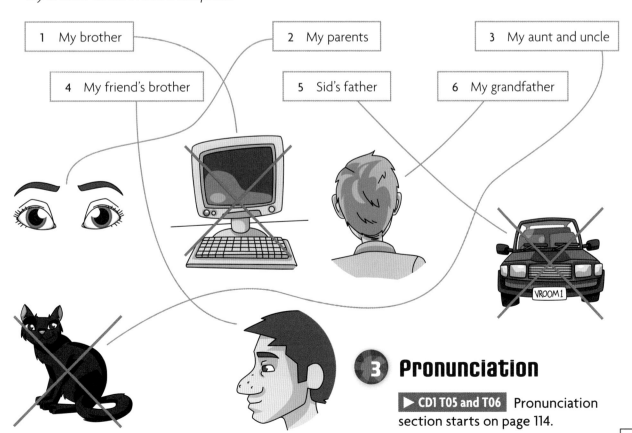

1 My brother	2 My parents	3 My aunt and uncle

4 My friend's brother	5 Sid's father	6 My grandfather

③ Pronunciation

▶ **CD1 T05 and T06** Pronunciation section starts on page 114.

4 Vocabulary

✱ Colors

a Write the colors.

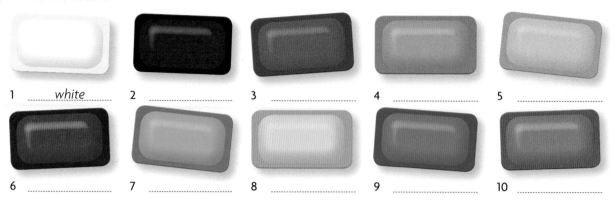

1 _white_ 2 _____ 3 _____ 4 _____ 5 _____

6 _____ 7 _____ 8 _____ 9 _____ 10 _____

b Work in a small group. Find something in your classroom that is each color.

The floor is white.   The computers are black.   The wall is brown.

✱ Rooms and furniture

c Look at the pictures. Write the names of the rooms (A–F).

d Look at the pictures. Label the furniture. Use the words in the box.

bathtub bed cabinet chair ~~door~~ fridge rug
sink shower sofa stove table toilet window

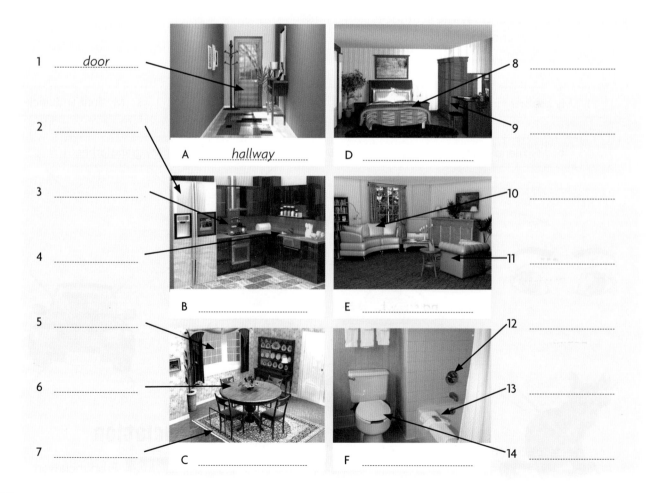

1 _door_

2 _____

3 _____

4 _____

5 _____

6 _____

7 _____

A _hallway_

B _____

C _____

D _____

E _____

F _____

8 _____

9 _____

10 _____

11 _____

12 _____

13 _____

14 _____

5 Grammar review
✳ There is / There are

a Complete the sentences. Use *There's a/an* or *There are*.

1 .... black table in the dining room.
2 .... two doors in our living room.
3 .... four white chairs in our kitchen.
4 .... three posters on the wall in my bedroom.
5 .... red chair in my sister's room.

b Play a memory game. Look at the picture for 30 seconds. Close your book. Then make sentences with *There's* or *There are*.

There are two windows.

6 Speak
✳ Prepositions of place

a Look at the picture again and say where things are. Use the prepositions in the box.

behind   between   in   next to   on   under

b Draw a floor plan of your house or apartment. Talk about it with your partner.

There are three bedrooms. There's a bathroom next to my parents' bedroom.
In the living room, there's a green sofa, and there are two brown chairs. The television is between ...
Where's the dining room?
It's next to the kitchen.

Culture in mind

7 Read and listen

a What's in your room? Check all the things that are in your room.

- ☐ a bed
- ☐ a desk or table
- ☐ a chair
- ☐ a sofa
- ☐ a rug
- ☐ a window
- ☐ a computer
- ☐ a TV

b Work with a partner. Look at the photos. Which room do you like the most? Why?

c ▶ CD1 T07 Read the text and listen. Then check (✓) the correct names in the chart. Sometimes more than one answer is possible.

		Vera	Kwan	Trish
1	has his/her own room	✓		✓
2	has a pink chair in his/her room			
3	has a clean room			
4	has a computer in his/her room			

More than a place to sleep

Many teenagers have the same favorite room at home – a bedroom! It's a place that is their own. They can do their homework, be with friends, read, listen to music or just relax in their bedrooms. Each teen's room is different. Meet these three teens and see what their rooms are like.

Vera

My room is great! It's big and clean. I have a blue rug in my room and a lot of white cabinets. On the wall, I have a poster of my favorite singer. My computer is under the poster, so I can look at it when I study! I have a lot of books in my room, too. I read a lot in my room. It's very quiet, and I like it that way.

Kwan

I share a room with my little brother. We have a small room, but it's cool. We keep it clean. Our room is red and blue. There are two beds, and there's a big window next to the beds. My brother is eight, and he likes cars. There are a lot of car posters on the wall. I don't like cars so much, but that's OK. I have four sisters, so I'm happy I have a room with my little brother. We go to our room a lot to get away!

Trish

I love my room! It's very messy, but that doesn't bother me. There are clothes on the floor and under my bed. My favorite thing in my room is my pink chair. My TV is great, too. The only problem: There are usually clothes on it!

These bedrooms are all different, but they have one thing in common: They show each person's personality. What is your room like?

8 Write

a Read Samir's description of his dream house. How many bedrooms are in his dream house? How many bathrooms?

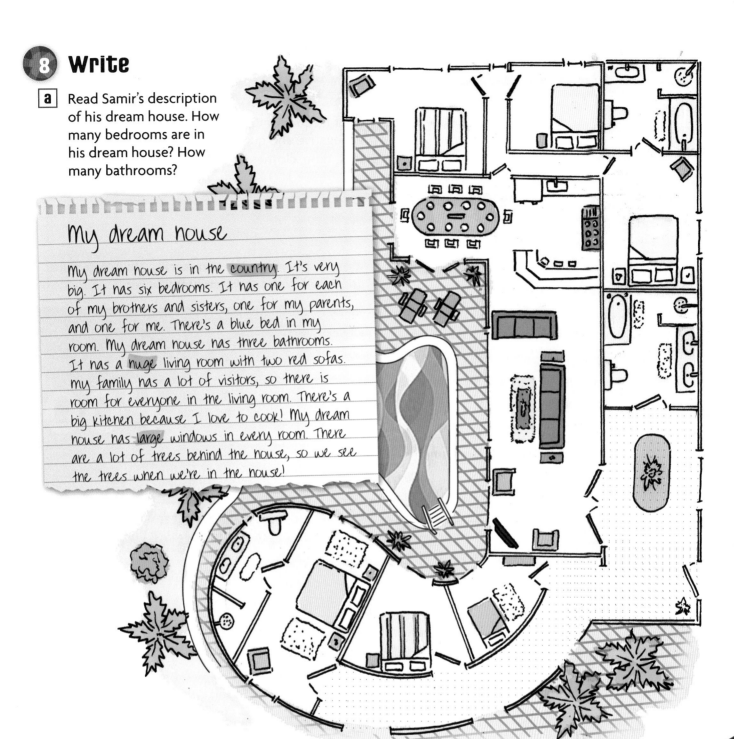

My dream house

My dream house is in the country. It's very big. It has six bedrooms. It has one for each of my brothers and sisters, one for my parents, and one for me. There's a blue bed in my room. My dream house has three bathrooms. It has a huge living room with two red sofas. My family has a lot of visitors, so there is room for everyone in the living room. There's a big kitchen because I love to cook! My dream house has large windows in every room. There are a lot of trees behind the house, so we see the trees when we're in the house!

b Write about your dream house and draw a floor plan. Include answers to these questions.

- What kind of house is it?
- Where is it?
- How many rooms does it have?
- How big are the rooms?
- What furniture is in some of the rooms?

9 Speak

a Work with a partner and describe your dream houses to each other. Ask each other questions about information that is not included in your writing or floor plan.

b Switch partners and describe your first partner's dream house. How much do you remember?

2 Some of the rules

* Grammar: Imperatives; Adverbs of frequency; Object pronouns; *can/can't* for ability; *There is / There are* (negative and questions) + *a/an/any*
* Vocabulary: Activity verbs, places, time, clothes, money and prices

1 Read and listen

✱ Activity verbs and imperatives

a Match the verbs to the pictures.

| close | cry | jump | laugh | listen | open |
| read | run | shout | smile | swim | write |

1 open
2 close 
3 run 
4 swim 
5 listen 
6 read 
7 jump 
8 laugh 
9 write 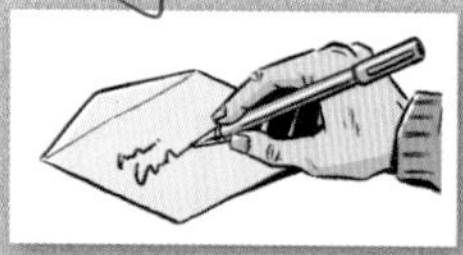
10 cry 
11 shout 
12 smile 

b Read the text quickly. How many rules are there at Westside Pool?

Westside Pool

Cost: $100 per month
$30 a week
$5 a day

Open from 8:00 a.m. – 7:00 p.m.

New members: Welcome to the Westside Pool.

Read our rules. Please follow them and make the pool fun and safe for everyone!

- Don't run by the pool.
- Close the doors when you enter the pool area.
- Swim in the swimming lanes.
- Don't jump into the pool from the side.
- Don't shout in the pool area.
- Listen to the lifeguards. 救生史

There are usually two lifeguards on duty. Tell them if you need help. You can also get help at the information desk. 讯问处，信息 资料

Thank you!

c ▶ CD1 T08 Now read the text again and listen. Circle the imperatives.

2 Grammar review

✱ Adverbs of frequency 频率 /fri:kwənsi/
词(副)

a Put the adverbs in the correct places in the diagram.

adj 正确的，恰当的.

always   hardly ever   sometimes   usually

100%					0%
1 always	2 usually	3 often	4 sometimes	5 hardly ever	6 never

LOOK!

We put the adverb of frequency:
– **after** the verb *be*, e.g. *I'm always late*
– **before** other verbs, e.g. *We always go to the movies on Friday.*

b Complete the sentences so they are true for you. Use *always, usually, often, sometimes, hardly ever* or *never*.

1 I __never__ play soccer after school.
2 My teachers __always__ give homework on Friday.
3 I __sometimes__ go to the movies on the weekend.
4 My best friend __hardly ever__ comes to my house on the weekend.
5 I'm __hardly ever__ late for school or work.

c Work with a partner. Talk about your sentences in Exercise 2b.

A: *I sometimes play soccer after school.*
B: *Really? I never play soccer after school. But I always play on the weekend.*

✱ Object pronouns review

Put the object pronoun in the sentences.

her   him   me   them   us   you

1 My mother really likes eggs, but I hate __them__.
2 Sara's my best friend. She calls __me__ every day.
3 My brother has a poster of Shakira. He really likes __her__.
4 Reynaldo is really nice. I really like __him__.
5 Do you have a problem with your homework? I can help __you__.
6 My sister and I like our uncle. He gives __us__ great birthday presents.

3 Pronunciation

▶ **CD1 T09 and T10** Pronunciation section starts on page 114.

4 Listen

✱ can/can't for ability

a ▶ **CD1 T11** Listen to Diego and Liz talking about what they can and can't do. Fill in the first two columns in the table.

✓✓ = Yes.   ✓ = Yes, but not very well.
✗ = No.

		Diego	Liz	You	Your partner
1					
2					
3					
4					

b Write sentences. Use the information in the table.

Diego can't swim. Liz can swim, but not very well.

c What about you? Fill in the column under *You* in the table.

d Work with a partner. Ask questions and fill in the last column of the table.

A: *Can you swim?*
B: *Yes, I can. Can you ... ?*

5 Vocabulary

* Places

Look at the pictures. What places do the pictures show? Write 1–8 in the boxes.

> 1 café   2 dance club   3 ~~movie theater~~   4 shoe store   5 bookstore
> 6 train station   7 clothing store   8 post office

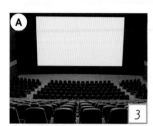 **A** 3

 **B** 6

 **C** 5

 **D** 2

 **E** 4

 **F** 1

 **G** 8

 **H** 7

6 Grammar review

* *There is / There are* (negative and questions) + *a/an/any*

a Complete the questions and short answers.

1 *Are there* any dance clubs here?

   (✗) No, there _____ .

2 _____ a train station in your town?

   (✓) Yes, there _____ .

3 _____ a post office on this street?

   (✓) Yes, _____ .

4 _____ any nice clothes in this store?

   (✗) No, _____ .

b Complete the sentences with *a* or *any*.

1 There aren't *any* good clothing stores here.

2 Is there _____ post office near here?

3 There's _____ good shoe store on this street.

4 Are there _____ bookstores in this town?

c What can you say about your city or town? Use the places in Exercise 5 and the questions and sentences in Exercises 6b and 6c to help you.

7 Speak

* Time

Look at the pictures. Make sentences.

1 *The post office opens at eight-thirty and closes at five-thirty.*

2 _____

3 _____

4 _____

5 _____

6 _____

8 Vocabulary

✳ Clothes

a Write the letters in the correct order to make words. Write them under the pictures.

sreds   skrit   hirst   scosk   ohess   ertewas   ~~siThrt~~   najse   scraf   reaensks   spatn   tekcaj

1 $24.00

T-shirt

2 $118.00

3 $89.75

4 $9.50

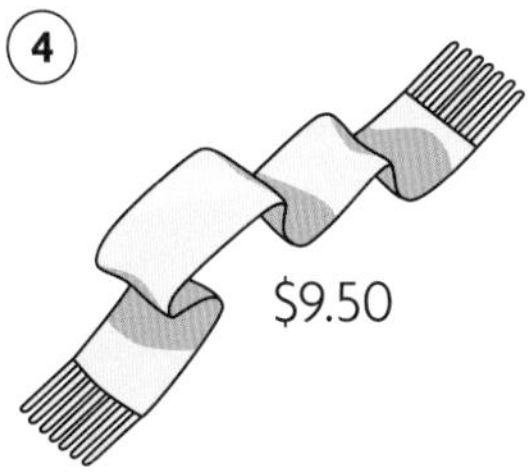

5 $5.25

6 $56.50

7 $195.00

8 $54.75

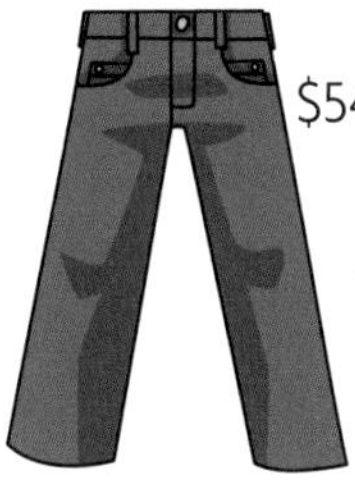

9 $47.99

10 $85.00

11 $62.99

12 $39.99

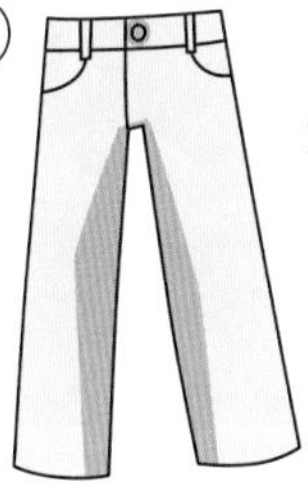

b Say what color the clothes are.

The T-shirt's blue.
The sneakers are purple.

c Work with a partner. Ask and answer.

A: _What color is your favorite shirt?_
B: _Blue. What color are your favorite shoes?_
A: _They're …_

LOOK!

We write $12.00 – we say _twelve dollars._

We write $7.25 – we say _seven dollars and twenty-five cents_ or _seven twenty-five._

We write $25.99 – we say _twenty-five dollars and ninety-nine cents_ or _twenty-five ninety-nine._

We write $125.00 – we say _a hundred and twenty-five dollars_ or _one hundred and twenty-five dollars._

9 Speak

✳ Money and prices

a ▶ CD1 T12 Work with a partner. Say the prices. Then listen and check your answers.

1 $12.00	4 $11.25
2 $25.00	5 $17.50
3 $125.00	6 $15.99

b Work with a partner. Say the prices of the clothes in Exercise 8a.

The T-shirt is twenty-four dollars.
The sneakers are eighty-nine seventy-five.

c Work with a partner. Ask and answer questions.

A: _How much is the T-shirt?_
B: _It's twenty-four dollars. How much are the sneakers?_

Too much homework

10 ▶ CD1 T13 **Read and listen**

a Look at the photostory. What do you think the problem is? Read and listen to find the solution to the problem.

1

Emily: Does anyone want to go to the movies tonight?

Alex: Sorry. I can't. I have too much homework.

Kim: Me, too. And it's so hard!

2

Matt: It's not that bad.

Kim: Yeah, not for you, but your older sister helps you!

Matt: True.

Kim: It's not fair! How will I ever get this all done?

3

Matt: Why don't we study together?

Emily: That's a great idea. We can go to the café.

Kim: Really? You guys would help me?

Alex: Wait, I need help, too. We can all help each other.

4

Kim: This was a good idea. We're almost done.

Alex: Great, now let's go to a movie!

Emily: Very funny! It's too late for that, Alex. But why don't we go on Friday?

Matt: Perfect! Let's plan on it.

b Complete the table. For each sentence, write a check in the column under the correct name.

	Matt	Emily	Kim	Alex
1 asks the group to go to a movie				
2 thinks the homework is hard				
3 doesn't think the homework is very hard				
4 suggests they study together				
5 says he needs help, too				
6 suggests they go to a movie on Friday				

11 Everyday English

a Find the expressions in the photostory. Who says them?

1 Really?

2 It's not that bad.

3 It's not fair!

4 Why don't we …

5 You guys

6 It's too late for that.

b Read the dialogue. Use the expressions in Exercise 11a to complete it.

Shelly: Hey, Leo. ¹........................... rent DVDs tonight?

Leo: I can't. I have to watch my brother.

Shelly: ²........................... ? You always have to watch him. ³...........................!

Leo: ⁴........................... . Actually, I like doing it.

Shelly: Hey, ⁵........................... can both come over. My parents will be home.

Leo: That's a good idea. We can rent a kid's movie.

Shelly: ⁶........................... . I have a scary movie already.

Leo: Oh, well, we can see that!

> ### Discussion box
>
> 1 Your friend invites you somewhere. You can't go. Say what happens.
>
> 2 Do you ever study or do homework with a group? Is it helpful?
>
> 3 How often do you help your friends? What do you do?

12 Improvisation

Work with a partner. Take two minutes to prepare a short role play. Do not write the text, just agree on your ideas for a short scene. Then act it out.

Roles: Kim and her dad

Situation: At Kim's house

Basic idea: Kim wants to go to a movie on Friday.

Use one of these sentences to start the conversation:

Kim: Can I go to the movies on Friday, Dad?

Dad: Let's go to dinner with your mom on Friday, Kim.

13 Reach Out ⊙ DVD Episode 1

a What's happening in the photo? What do you think his summer job is?

b Match the words to the meanings. Then watch Episode 1 and meet Alex, Emily, Matt and Kim.

1 glad   a a person who creates clothes

2 realize   b understand

3 tough   c marks you get at school

4 semester   d hard, difficult

5 grades   e part of the school year

6 fashion designer   f happy

14 Write

Hi, Anna!

How are you? I'm glad you want to join the book club, Book It.
It's a fun group. We read a book each week. There is a meeting
on Wednesday. We sometimes watch movies of the books we read
on Fridays. We have a few rules.

- Read the book before the meeting.
- Ask and answer questions about the book.
- Be polite. Listen to others.
- Don't shout. (We meet in a bookstore, so we need to be quiet!)
- Laugh and smile!

That's it! It's a really fun club. I hope you can come on Wednesday.
See you,
Mario

a Read Mario's email to Anna about the book club. Answer the questions.

1 What's the name of the club?

2 What does the club do on Fridays?

3 Where does the club meet?

b Think of a club or a group you are in that has rules. Write an email to a friend telling him/her about it.

15 Last but not least: more speaking

Work with a partner. Imagine you have a business.
Decide on the following together:

- The type of business: a bookstore, a movie theater or a dance club
- A name for your business
- How much items cost (books and magazines, tickets, snacks, entrance fee, food)
- The rules at your business

For your portfolio

Check your progress

1 Grammar

a Complete the sentences. Choose the correct words.

1 Where is _____ family from?

   a you   b your   c he

2 Ahmed _____ three sisters.

   a to have   b have   c has

3 _____ a rug under the table.

   a There is   b Is there   c There are

4 _____ potatoes in the refrigerator?

   a Are there any   b Is there any
   c Is there a

5 Tomoko and Dan _____ from Japan.

   a is   b be   c are

6 _____ the door, please.

   a Close   b Closes   c Close to

   [6]

b Complete the sentences. (Circle) the correct words.

1 I like soccer. I (*can / can't*) play very well.

2 This is David's book. Please give it to (*her / him*).

3 How many brothers do you (*be / have*)?

4 The sofa is (*next to / between*) the table.

5 (*Don't run / Run*) by the pool. It's dangerous.

6 I (*never / always*) do my homework, but my sister doesn't.

7 Is there (*a / an*) chair in your bedroom?

8 (*There is / There are*) two computers in my room.

   [8]

2 Vocabulary

a Write the words and phrases in the lists.

> bathtub   black   blue   café   dress
> green   jacket   pants   post office
> purple   shoe store   sink   skirt
> sofa   table   train station

Colors	Places
....	....
....	....
....	....
....	

Clothes	Furniture
....	....
....	....
....	....
....	....

   [16]

b Use the words in the box to complete the sentences.

> 10:00 $28.00   bedroom
> dining room   Open   swim

1 I have a big bed in my _____ .

2 The movie is at _____ .

3 I can't _____ very well.

4 _____ your books to page 10.

5 The skirt is _____ .

6 We have a big table and four chairs in the _____ .

   [6]

How did you do?

Check your score.

Total score	🙂 Very good	😐 OK	🙁 Not very good
36			
Grammar	14 – 11	10 – 9	8 or less
Vocabulary	22 – 18	17 – 15	14 or less

* Simple present (affirmative and negative; questions and short answers)
* *like + -ing*
* Vocabulary: hobbies and interests, school subjects

1 Read and listen

a Look at the pictures. How old do you think the girl is? What is her hobby? Read the text quickly to check your ideas.

b ► CD1 T14 Now read the text again and listen. Answer the questions.

1 Where is Kellie from?
2 Why does she feed the bees in the winter?
3 When does she get honey from the hives?
4 What does she do with the honey?
5 Why don't her friends go near the hives?

An unusual hobby

Kellie Lenamond is 16. She's from Texas in the United States. She has many hobbies. She likes playing volleyball. She also likes playing the fiddle, and she loves singing. But, Kellie has an unusual hobby: beekeeping.

Kellie doesn't work with the bees every day. She checks her hives about twice a month in the spring, summer and fall. She spends more time with the bees in the winter. There aren't many flowers for the bees to get food from at this time of year. So, Kellie feeds the bees a mixture of sugar and water in the winter.

 Kellie has six beehives. She has about 360,000 bees!

This is a typical day for Kellie when she works with the bees:

8:00	She gets up and eats breakfast.
9:00	She sets out her beesuit. She makes sugar water for the bees.
11:00	She practices the fiddle.
12:00	She makes lunch for her brothers and sisters. Then she does her homework.
3:00	She goes to volleyball practice.
5:00	She and her mom make dinner.
7:00	After dinner, Kellie puts on her beesuit. She and her dad go to the backyard. She feeds the bees the sugar water.

Kellie's friends don't go near the hives. They are afraid. They don't want the bees to sting them. Kellie says they don't understand that bees are a good thing. She says, "I like standing safely in the middle of a swirling mass of stinging insects. No one else is brave enough!"

Every summer, Kellie takes honey from the hives. Her bees produce about 35 liters of honey a year. Kellie and her family sell some of the honey, cook with the honey and give friends honey, too.

② Grammar

✳ Simple present (affirmative and negative)

a Look at the examples. Then complete the rule.

*Kellie **gets up** at 8:00.*
*She **feeds** the bees.*
*The bees **produce** honey.*
*They **cook** with honey.*

> **RULE:** We use the simple present for things which happen regularly or which are always true.
>
> With *I*, _____ , *we* and _____ we use the base form of the verb. With *he*, *she* and *it* we add _____ .

⌕LOOK!

With *he*, *she* and *it*, some verbs end in *es*.

-sh   they wash – she wash**es**

-ch   we teach – he teach**es**,
         I go – she go**es**

If the verb ends with consonant + *y*, the ending is *ies*.

they fly – it fl**ies**

you study – he stud**ies**

b Complete the sentences. Use the simple present form of the verbs.

1   Sara ___*loves*___ (love) movies.

2   My friends _____ (hate) sports.

3   You _____ (take) good photographs.

4   Mrs. Jameson _____ (teach) us English.

5   My father _____ (fly) to Chile twice a year.

6   My mom _____ (read) a lot of books.

7   We _____ (go) to school at 8:30 in the morning.

c Look at the pictures. Write simple present sentences. Use *like*, *love* or *hate* and a word from the box.

> cats   soccer   ~~apples~~   ice cream   bananas   winter

1   He *likes apples.*

2   I _____ .

3   She _____ .

4   They _____ .

5   She _____ .

6   We _____ .

d Look at the examples and complete the table.

*Kellie **doesn't work** with the bees every day.*
*They **don't go** near the hives.*

Affirmative	Negative
I/you/we/they **run**	I/you/we/they _____ (**do not**) run
he/she/it **runs**	he/she/it _____ (**does not**) run

e Complete the sentences. Use the simple present form of the verbs.

1   I ___*don't like*___ (not like) this kind of music.

2   We _____ (not eat) a lot of meat at home.

3   My parents _____ (speak) Spanish.

4   I _____ (not know) his phone number.

5   My brother _____ (get up) late on the weekend.

6   My father _____ (not drive) to work.

f Make the sentences negative.

1 My brother spends a lot of money on clothes.

My brother doesn't spend a lot of money on clothes.

2 I get up early on Sunday.

....

3 My sister watches a lot of TV.

....

4 I buy music on that Web site.

....

5 You know the answer.

....

3 **Vocabulary**

✳ Hobbies and interests

a ▶ **CD1 T15** Match the activities with the pictures. Write 1–9 in the boxes. Then listen, check and repeat.

1 going to the movies
2 reading
3 swimming
4 painting
5 playing computer games
6 dancing
7 listening to music
8 playing the guitar
9 running

b Use words from the three lists to make five true sentences.

	play	
	plays	
	don't play	
	doesn't play	magazines.
I	listen to	the guitar.
My friends	doesn't listen to	pop music.
My brother	go	computer games.
My sister	goes	tennis.
	doesn't go	to soccer games.
	read	a newspaper every day.
	don't read	
	doesn't read	

4 Grammar

✳ *like + -ing*

a Look at the examples and complete the rule.

*Kellie likes **playing** the fiddle.*
*She loves **singing**.*
*We enjoy **cooking** with honey.*
*I hate **getting** up early!*

> **RULE:** We often use the .... form after verbs of liking and not liking, for example, *like*, *don't like*, *love* and *hate*.

⌕ LOOK!

If the verb ends in *e*, we drop the *e* before *-ing*.
dance – dancing, smile – smiling

If a short verb ends in vowel + consonant, we double the last letter before *-ing*.
swim – swi**mm**ing, run – ru**nn**ing

b Complete the sentences. Use the *-ing* form of the verbs in the box.

> ride   run   play   go   ~~listen~~   talk

1 Maria hates ___*listening*___ to jazz.
2 My brother doesn't like .... games.
3 My sister loves .... her bike.
4 My dad enjoys .... on the beach.
5 I love .... to my friends on the phone.
6 We love .... to soccer games on the weekend.

5 Speak

a Work with a partner. Talk about the hobbies in Exercise 3.

I love …   I (don't) like/enjoy …
I hate …   I'm (not) good at …

b Make notes and tell other people in your class about your partner's hobbies.

6 Listen

a ▶ CD1 T16   Listen to the interview. Which picture shows Mark's hobby?

① ② ③

b ▶ CD1 T16   Listen again. Write *T* (true) or *F* (false).

1 Mark gives shows once a month. ☐
2 He learns new tricks on the Internet. ☐
3 Mark practices every day. ☐
4 Mark's brother wants to be a magician. ☐

7 Pronunciation

▶ CD1 T17 and T18   Pronunciation section starts on page 114.

8 Grammar

✳ Simple present (questions and short answers)

a Read the examples about Mark's hobby and complete the table.

*Do your friends **know** about your hobby? Yes, they **do**.*
*Does it **take** a long time to learn? Yes, it **does**.*
*Do you **tell** your brother how to do the tricks?*

Questions	Short answers
.... I/you/we/they study English?	Yes, I/you/we/they **do**. No, I/you/we/they .... (do not).
.... he/she/it like studying English?	Yes, he/she/it .... No, he/she/it **doesn't** (............ not).

*No, I **don't**.*

b Complete the questions and short answers.

1 A: ___*Does*___ Jeremy like swimming?
   B: ___*Yes, he does*_____ (✓) .
2 A: .... you study Japanese?
   B: .... (✗) .
3 A: .... your friends listen to music?
   B: .... (✓) .
4 A: .... she go to your school?
   B: .... (✓) .

Culture in mind

9 Read and listen

a Tonya, Elsa and Mark go to the same school. Read the text quickly and find:

1 the name of the school
2 three different clubs at the school

b Look at the pictures. Which things are school subjects? Which things are clubs? Which are sports? Write *S* (subject), *C* (club) or *SP* (sport).

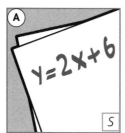
A — Y = 2x + 6 — S

B

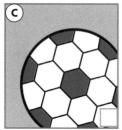
C

D

E

F

G — Español

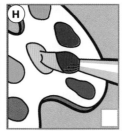
H

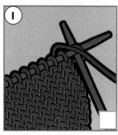
I

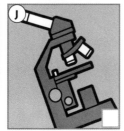
J

School life

Tonya, Elsa and Mark are students at LaGuardia High School in New York City. It's a school with regular academic classes, but it also specializes in the performing arts. Tonya likes dancing, Elsa wants to be an artist and Mark is a singer.

The students are all 15, and they're in 10th grade. They study subjects like English, math, social studies, science, health and PE. They also choose a foreign language: French, Italian, Spanish or Japanese. Students have many academic classes, but during the school day they also take classes in the arts, like theater, art, dance and music. Mark says, "I get the basic classes, but I also take a voice class and a music history class."

There is even more for LaGuardia students after school. There are more than 40 clubs for students. For example, there's a movie club, a knitting club and an environment club. "We have so many choices here," says Tonya. "My favorite club is the camera club. I like taking photos and learning about photography. It's also a great way to meet people with common interests."

Students at LaGuardia can also do many sports. For example, they can play basketball, tennis, volleyball and soccer. Elsa is on the gymnastics team. She says, "I like being on a team. It makes me work hard and do my best." Students practice after school. They compete against other high schools. Mark says, "At school, I study by myself. I'm a singer, and I do that alone, too. That's why I like playing on the basketball team. We work together and compete against other teams."

LaGuardia offers many great classes, clubs and sports for students. Students at LaGuardia get a good education, and they also develop their own interests. Many LaGuardia students become dancers, singers and actors!

10 Write

a Imagine that Lisa is your new e-pal and this is her first message to you. Read her message. What are her hobbies and interests?

from: lisa.franklin@aeim.cup

subject: Hello!

Hi!

I'm Lisa Franklin. I'm American, and I live in California. I'm 15.

I love sports. My favorite hobby is painting. I also like taking photographs (I'm in the photography club at school), and I enjoy riding my bike. I love watching sports on TV, especially tennis! I really like Rafael Nadal.

My best friend is Sonia. We listen to music a lot, and we often go to the movies together, too. Her favorite actor is Ben Stiller. I think he's very funny, but my favorite actor is Johnny Depp.

Write soon!

Lisa

c ▶ **CD1 T19** Read the text again and listen. Write *T* (true) or *F* (false).

1 Tonya, Elsa and Mark are all 15 years old. ☐
2 Mark is a dancer. ☐
3 Art classes are school subjects at LaGuardia. ☐
4 Clubs meet during the school day. ☐
5 Tonya's favorite club is the movie club. ☐
6 Elsa is on the gymnastics team. ☐
7 Mark sings in a band with other people. ☐
8 Sports teams compete against other teams. ☐

d Is this school similar to yours or very different? Discuss this question with a partner or in small groups.

b Write an email in reply to Lisa. Include this information:

- your name, nationality and age
- where you live
- your hobbies and interests
- some information about your friend(s)

11 Speak

a Work with a partner. Think of five questions that you would like to ask Tonya from LaGuardia High School.

b Work with your partner: One of you is the interviewer, and the other one is Tonya. Ask and answer questions.

For your portfolio

4 Helping other people

* Present continuous for activities happening now
* Simple present vs. present continuous
* Vocabulary: housework

1 Read and listen

a Give any examples you can of people who do "volunteer work" (work you do without being paid).

b Look at the photos. How old do you think Mike is? Where is he, and what is he doing? Read the text quickly and check your ideas.

c ▶ CD1 T20 Read the text again and listen. Mark the statements *T* (true) or *F* (false).

1 Mike usually lives in Nebraska. ☐

2 Mike is studying to become a doctor. ☐

3 Mike is unhappy because he doesn't get any money. ☐

4 Mike is living in a house with five other people. ☐

5 Mike wants to go home when he finishes his work. ☐

d Answer the questions.

1 Why does Mike like what he is doing?

2 Say three places in the world where you would like to work as a volunteer.

3 Give an example of: a) volunteer work you would like to do; b) volunteer work you would not like to do.

Helping at a hospital

Every year many young people finish school and then take a year off before they start work or go to college. Some of them go to other countries and work as volunteers. Volunteers give their time to help people. For example, they work in schools or hospitals, or they help with conservation.

Mike Coleman is 19 and lives in Omaha, Nebraska, in the United States. He wants to become a teacher, but now he's living in Namibia. He's working in a hospital near Katima Mulilo. He says, "I'm working with the doctors and nurses here to help sick people. I'm not a doctor but I can do a lot of things to help. For example, I help carry people who can't walk. Sometimes I go to villages in the mobile hospital, too. There aren't many doctors here so they need help from people like me. I don't get any money, but that's OK, I'm not here for the money."

"I'm staying here for two months, and I'm living in a small house with five other volunteers. The work is hard and the days are long, but I'm enjoying my life here. I'm learning a lot about life in southern Africa, and about myself! When I finish the two months' work, I want to travel in and around Namibia for three weeks. For example, I want to see the animals in the Okavango Delta in Botswana."

ANGOLA ZAMBIA

Katima Mulilo ☐

NAMIBIA

Windhoek BOTSWANA

SOUTH AFRICA

2 Grammar

✳ Present continuous for activities happening now

RULE: We use the present _____ to talk about things that are happening at or around the time of speaking.

We form the present _____ with the present tense of _____ + verb + *ing*.

a Look at the examples. Then complete the rule and the table.

*He's **working** in a hospital near Katima Mulilo.*
*I'm **living** in a small house with five other volunteers.*
*I'm **learning** a lot about life in southern Africa.*

Affirmative	Negative	Questions	Short answers
I'm (am) work**ing**	I'm **not** work**ing**	_____ I work**ing**?	Yes, I **am**. No, I'm **not**.
you/we/they**'re** (_____) work**ing**	you/we/they **aren't** work**ing**	_____ you/we/they work**ing**?	Yes, you/we/they _____ . No, you/we/they _____ .
he/she/it**'s (is)** work**ing**	he/she/it _____ work**ing**	_____ he/she/it work**ing**?	Yes, he/she/it _____ . No, he/she/it _____ .

b Complete the sentences. Use the present continuous form of the verbs.

1 Sorry, Eddie isn't here. He *'s taking* (take) the dog for a walk.
2 Mike and Jane are in the living room. They _____ (watch) a movie on DVD.
3 Hannah! You _____ (not listen) to me!
4 I can't talk now. I _____ (do) my homework.
5 A: _____ you _____ (watch) this show? B: No, I'm not. Watch a different one if you want.
6 A: Maddy's upstairs in her room. B: Oh? Really? _____ she _____ (take) a nap?

c Look at the pictures and complete the sentences with the present continuous. Use the phrases in the box.

listen to music   win   ~~take a nap~~   not enjoy this show   not do her homework   watch television

1 My grandfather
   is taking a nap .

2 Look! Our dog Max
   _____ !

3 My parents
   _____ .

4 I _____ .

5 It's a great game, and
   we _____ !

6 Ellie _____ .

3 Pronunciation

> **CD1 T21 and T22** Pronunciation section starts on page 114.

4 Grammar

✱ Simple present vs. present continuous

a Look at the examples. Then (circle) the correct words in the sentences.

Simple Present	Present Continuous
*Mike **lives** in Omaha, Nebraska.*	*He's **living** in a house in Namibia right now.*
*Many people **work** as volunteers.*	*Mike **is working** in a hospital right now.*
*It often **snows** here.*	*Look outside. It's **snowing**!*

1 *We (always wear) / We're always wearing* a uniform to school.

2 *Paula wears / Paula's wearing* black jeans today.

3 Come inside! *It rains / It's raining.*

4 *It rains / It's raining* a lot in February.

5 *Dad cooks / Dad's cooking* right now.

6 *My mother cooks / My mother's cooking* lunch every Sunday.

7 Steve's terrible! *He never listens / He's never listening* to the teacher!

LOOK!

These verbs are almost never used in the present continuous:

believe   know   understand   want
remember   need   mean   like   hate

I **know** the answer. (Not: ~~I'm knowing~~.)
My friend **likes** rap music. (Not: ~~My friend is liking~~.)

b We use different time expressions with the two tenses. Complete the lists with the time expressions in the box.

> right now   usually   every weekend
> this afternoon   never   today
> every evening   this week   twice a year

Simple present	Present continuous
every day	now
always	this morning
....	....
....	....
....	....
....	....

c Complete the sentences. Use the simple present or present continuous form of the verbs.

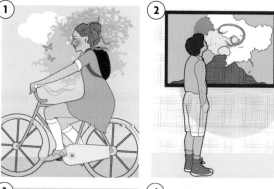

1 Sarah usually __walks__ (walk) to school, but today she .... (ride) her bike.

2 We .... (have) geography class twice a week. We .... (learn) about volcanoes right now.

3 Julia .... (surf) the Net this afternoon. She .... (want) to find some information for a project.

4 I .... (know) his face, but I .... (not remember) his name.

5 We .... (not dance) tonight because we .... (not like) the music.

6 What .... this word .... (mean)? I .... (not understand) it.

5 Listen

a ▶ **CD1 T23** Listen to a radio interview with Mike Coleman. What is he doing at the time of the interview? Choose the correct picture.

b ▶ **CD1 T23** Listen again and write *T* (true) or *F* (false).

1 Mike has breakfast at around eight o'clock. ☐
2 Mike and his friends make breakfast, lunch and dinner. ☐
3 Mike uses a washing machine to do the laundry. ☐
4 Mike sometimes cleans the floors and washes the windows at the hospital. ☐
5 Mike is working with boring people. ☐

6 Vocabulary

❋ Housework

▶ **CD1 T24** Match the words with the pictures. Write 1–7 in the boxes. Then listen, check and repeat.

1 cook
2 iron the clothes
3 do the laundry
4 go grocery shopping
5 do the dishes
6 clean up / clean a room
7 wash the windows

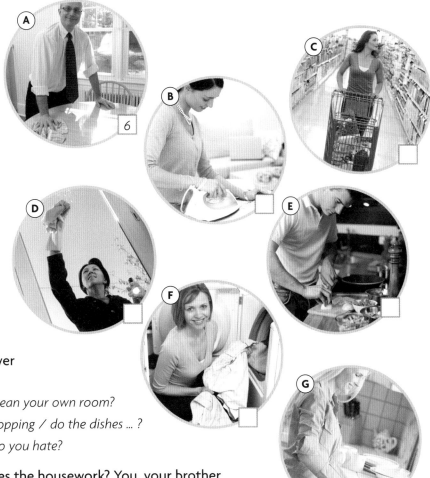

7 Speak

a Work in a group. Ask and answer questions about housework.

Do you help at home? Do you clean your own room?
How often do you go grocery shopping / do the dishes ... ?
Which jobs do you like? Which do you hate?

b In your home, who usually does the housework? You, your brother or sister, your mother, your father? Compare with a partner.

My father usually cooks, but my mother always does the dishes ...

Let's help him out.

a Look at the photostory. What do Emily, Alex and Matt do? Why do you think Kim doesn't help? Read and listen to find the answers.

①

②

Emily: Hey, look at that guy.

Matt: Yeah. Let's help him out. Come on, Kim.

Kim: Not me. It's not my problem. Let *him* push his own car.

Alex: Well, I'm going to help him.

③

Matt: Come on! One, two, three – push!

Emily: Wow, it's heavy!

Alex: Yes, it is. It's moving, though!

Matt: We did it!

Alex: But he drove away! And he didn't even say thank you!

Matt: Hey, that's right. That's not very nice, is it?

④

Kim: See? I told you! You guys are crazy.

Emily: Why?

Kim: Oh, come on, Emily! The man didn't even say thank you!

Emily: So what? We pushed the car to *help* him, not to hear him say thank you.

b Match the beginnings and endings to make a summary of the story.

1	A man	a	want to help him.
2	Matt, Alex and Emily	b	but he doesn't say thank you.
3	Kim thinks	c	needs help to start his car.
4	The car is heavy, but	d	that "thank you" isn't important.
5	The man drives away	e	they push it and it starts.
6	Emily thinks	f	that it's the man's problem, not hers.

9 Everyday English

a Find expressions 1–6 in the photostory. Who says them?

1 It's not my problem.
2 Come on!
3 ..., though.
4 That's right.
5 See?
6 So what?

b Read the dialogue. Use the expressions in Exercise 9a to complete it.

Linda: What time does the movie start? Eight o'clock?

Paul: [1] *That's right* .

Linda: Well, we're late. [2] _____ , Paul! Let's go.

Paul: Late? No, we aren't late. Look at my watch. [3] _____ ? It's only six thirty.

Linda: Oh, yes. OK, so we don't need to leave now. I don't want to be late, [4] _____ . Everyone says it's a really good movie! And Ashton Kutcher's in it.

Paul: [5] _____ ? Ashton Kutcher isn't very good!

Linda: Not very good? You just don't understand acting. Well, [6] _____ . You don't have to come!

Discussion box

1 Kim says the others are "crazy" because they helped the driver. What is your opinion?

2 In what situations do you find it easy or difficult to ask other people for help? Give your reasons.

3 When did you last help someone who had a problem? Say what happened.

10 Improvisation

Work with a partner. Take two minutes to prepare a short role play. Try to use some of the expressions from Exercise 9a. Do not write the text, just agree on your ideas for a short scene. Then act it out.

Roles: Kim and the car driver

Situation: On the street, the next day

Basic idea: Kim and the driver see each other on the street the next day.

Use one of these sentences to start the conversation:

Kim: Excuse me, I think I know you. We helped you push your car yesterday.

Man: Hi! Can I talk to you for a minute? I'd just like to say I'm sorry ...

11 Reach Out ● DVD Episode 2

a What's happening in the situation in the photo? What is the teacher going to say?

b Match the words with their definitions. Then watch Episode 2 and see what happens with Emily, Matt, Kim and Alex.

1 community outreach project
2 senior center
3 semester
4 guest
5 bracelet
6 to joke

a to say something and not be serious about it
b a person who comes to a place because they are invited
c a piece of jewelry worn around the wrist or arm
d a school project that involves working without pay to help other people
e a place for older people to do activities
f part of the school year, usually half

12 Write

a Read Maggie's email to her friend about a family party. Answer the questions.

1 What is the event and when is it happening?
2 How many people are coming?
3 What is everybody doing to help?

b Imagine you are helping to prepare for one of these events:

● a family party
● a birthday celebration for one of your friends
● a good-bye party for your teacher

Write an email to a friend and tell him/her what is happening.

Hi, Joanna!

How are things? I hope you're well.

This is going to be a quick message because I'm really busy. We're getting ready for my sister's 18th birthday. There's going to be a big party in the backyard tonight. About 50 people are coming! So we're all here, cleaning and cooking. My mom's in the kitchen preparing food, and my dad's helping her. My sister Jill and my brother Brad are putting up a big tent and some lights in the backyard, and some of my sister's friends are putting out the tables and chairs. My grandparents aren't helping. They're taking a nap in their room. Well, sorry, I have to go. My mom's calling me. She needs some help!

Have a good weekend!

See you soon.

Maggie

---

13 Last but not least: more speaking

a ▶ **CD1 T26** Read the phone call between Monique and her friend Tanya. Complete the dialogue using the verbs in the box in their correct form. Then listen and check.

> study   ~~speak~~   help   do   think   clean

Monique: Hi! Is Tanya there?

Tanya: Yes. This is Tanya _speaking_ .

Monique: Oh, hi! How are you?

Tanya: I'm OK. I'm a little busy right now.

Monique: Busy? What are you [1] _____ ?

Tanya: Well, I'm [2] _____ my brother with his math homework, but I'm also [3] _____ my room ...

Monique: What else?

Tanya: I'm [4] _____ about what I can get Jim for his birthday.

Monique: You know what, Tanya? Let's meet at the mall in half an hour and go shopping together. We can look for a present for Jim.

Tanya: Sorry, Monique, I can't.

Monique: No? Why not?

Tanya: I'm also [5] _____ for my English test. It's tomorrow!

Monique: Oh, no!

b Look at the dialogue with a partner. Think of some changes to make to the dialogue (names, for example), so that it becomes your dialogue. Act out the new dialogue in pairs. (Don't just read it aloud!)

Check your progress

1 Grammar

a Complete the sentences. Use the simple present form of the verbs.

1 You should read more, Jane. You _watch_ (watch) too much TV.

2 My uncle _____ (live) in that house over there.

3 _____ you _____ (like) listening to music?

4 Alex and Sarah _____ (play) computer games every weekend.

5 My father _____ (not like) the same music as me.

6 Our teacher hardly ever _____ (give) us a lot of homework.

7 A: _____ your mother _____ (work) on Saturdays?

   B: Yes, she _____ .

8 A: _____ they _____ (write) a lot of emails?

   B: No, they _____ .

9 I _____ (not get up) early on the weekend. | 10 |

b Complete the sentences. Use the simple present or present continuous form of the verbs.

1 Annie often _plays_ (play) soccer, but now she _'s playing_ (play) computer games.

2 My mom usually _____ (work) in Chicago, but this week she _____ (work) in New York.

3 I _____ (read) a magazine right now. It's strange, because I _____ usually _____ (not read) magazines.

4 We _____ (not watch) television very often, but we _____ (watch) an interesting show right now.

5 A: _____ your friends always _____ (swim) in the ocean?

   B: No, not always. They _____ (swim) in the pool today.

6 A: Karen's not in her room. _____ she _____ (help) Dad in the kitchen?

   B: No, she _____ (be) . She _____ (take) a shower. | 11 |

2 Vocabulary

a Put the letters in order to find nine more school subjects.

1 usmci _____music_____

2 marda _____

3 thma _____

4 shinglE _____

5 niecsec _____

6 orthiys _____

7 nSipahs _____

8 aggyehorp _____

9 logonyetch _____

10 yescmtrih _____ | 9 |

b Write the words and phrases in the lists. Then add three more to each list.

ironing the clothes   ~~listening to music~~
dancing   washing the windows
cleaning up   playing the guitar

Hobbies and interests	Housework
listening to music	

| 11 |

How did you do?

Check your score.

Total score	🙂	😐	🙁
41	Very good	OK	Not very good
Grammar	21 – 17	16 – 14	13 or less
Vocabulary	20 – 16	15 – 13	12 or less

Who's your hero?

* Simple past: *be* and regular verbs (affirmative and negative), *was born / were born*
* Vocabulary: multi-word verbs (1), memory words

1 Read and listen

a Look at the photos and the title. Why do you think this woman is a hero for some people? Read the text quickly and check your ideas.

Erin Brockovich

Erin Brockovich, an American woman, was born in Kansas. She studied at a business college for a year, and then she moved to southern California and married a restaurant manager.

In 1990, when she was 30 years old, she was in a car accident. A law company helped her after the accident, and later she started to work for them.

Her job was to organize papers. One day Erin realized that there were lots of papers about some very sick people in a place called Hinkley. She started to look for more information about the town.

Erin worked very hard for five years. She visited lots of sick people in Hinkley and listened to their stories. All the people lived near a big Pacific Gas and Electric factory, and she discovered that there was a chemical called chromium in the local water. It was from the factory, and Erin believed that the people were sick because of the chromium in their drinking water. She planned to help them.

Erin and her boss started a law case against the Pacific Gas and Electric company. The company wasn't happy about this. They didn't agree that the people were sick because of the water. In 1996, the judge ordered Pacific Gas and Electric to pay the people in Hinkley $500,000 each (there were 600 sick people, so that was $333 million in total).

In 2000, there was a movie about Erin Brockovich. Julia Roberts played Erin, and the movie was very successful. Now Erin is famous. She has her own company, and she gives talks all over the world.

b ▶ **CD1 T27** Now read the text again and listen. Answer the questions.

1 What was Erin's job at the law company?
2 Why did Erin start to look for more information about Hinkley?
3 Where did the sick people in Hinkley live?
4 What was Erin's theory about why the people were sick?
5 How much money did Pacific Gas and Electric pay to people in Hinkley?
6 What does Erin Brockovich do now?

c Do you think the people in Hinkley were happy with the result of the law case?

② Grammar

✳ Simple past: *be*

a Look at the text on page 30. Underline examples of the simple past of the verb *be*.

b Complete the table.

Affirmative	Negative	Question	Short answer
I/he/she/it **was**	I/he/she/it _____ (was not)	_____ I/he/she/it?	Yes, I/he/she/it _____ . No, I/he/she/it _____ (was not).
you/we/they **were**	you/we/they _____ (were not)	_____ you/we/they?	Yes, you/we/they _____ . No, you/we/they _____ (were not).

c Complete the sentences with *was*, *wasn't*, *were* or *weren't*.

1 In 1990, Erin ____*was*____ in a car accident.

2 A lot of people in Hinkley _____ sick.

3 The drinking water in Hinkley _____ clean.

4 There _____ chromium in the water.

5 The bosses at Pacific Gas and Electric _____ happy.

d Complete the questions with *Was* or *Were*.

1 ____*Was*____ Erin Brockovich British?

2 _____ it her job to drive a car for the law company?

3 _____ there lots of papers about sick people in Hinkley?

4 _____ the water in Hinkley clean?

5 _____ a lot of people in Hinkley sick?

6 _____ the movie *Erin Brockovich* successful?

e Work with a partner. Ask and answer the questions in Exercise 2d.

A: *Was Erin Brockovich British?*
B: *No, she wasn't. She was American.*

③ Pronunciation

▶ **CD1 T28, T29 and T30** Pronunciation section starts on page 114.

④ Grammar

✳ *was born / were born*

Look at the example. Complete the sentences with your information.

Erin Brockovich was born in 1960. She was born in the U.S.

1 I was born in _____ (year).

2 I was born in _____ (place).

⑤ Speak

a Ask other students.

When were you born?
Where were you born?

b Work with a partner. Ask and answer about family members. Complete the table for your partner's family.

A: *When was your sister born?*
B: *In 1998. Where were your parents born?*
A: *My mother was born in Rome, and my father …*

Name	Year	Place
Grandfather		

6 Grammar

✱ Simple past: regular verbs

a Look back at the text on page 30. Find the simple past form of these verbs.

study   _studied_

marry   ....

help   ....

start   ....

realize   ....

visit   ....

live   ....

believe   ....

plan   ....

order   ....

b Look at the verbs in Exercise 6a. Complete the rule.

> **RULE:** We use the simple past to talk about finished actions in the past.
>
> With regular verbs, we usually add .... to the verb (_work – worked, start – started_).
>
> If the verb ends in _e_ (for example, _live_), we add ....
>
> If a short verb ends in one vowel + consonant (for example, _plan_), we double the .... and add _ed_.
>
> If the verb ends in consonant + _y_ (for example, _study_), we change the _y_ to .... and add ....

c Complete the sentences. Use the simple past form of the verbs.

1 Last night, I _studied_ (study) for today's test.

2 There was no food in the house, so we .... (order) a pizza.

3 I .... (want) to go to the movies, and my friend Alex .... (agree) to come with me.

4 I .... (try) to call my friend on Saturday, but no one .... (answer).

5 Last year we .... (visit) my aunt and uncle in Australia.

6 My father .... (stop) watching TV and .... (help) me with my homework.

d Look at the example and complete the table.

The company **didn't agree** that the people were sick because of the water.

Affirmative	Negative
I/you/he/she/it/we/they want**ed**	I/you/he/she/it/we/they .... want

e Complete the sentences. Use the simple past form of the verbs in the box.

> ~~start~~   talk   clean   stay   rain   study   not wash
> ~~not finish~~   not like   not watch   not play   not say

1 I _started_ a painting, but I _didn't finish_ it.

2 They .... in an expensive hotel, but they .... the food.

3 It .... all day on Saturday, so we .... tennis.

4 Maria .... TV last night. She .... for her test.

5 I .... my room, but I .... the windows.

6 He .... for a long time, but he .... anything interesting!

7 Listen

a Josh made a poster about his hero for a class presentation. Look at the poster and the sentences. How many of the sentences can you complete?

b ▶ CD1 T31 Listen to Josh's presentation. Find information to complete the other sentences in the poster.

c Why is Dorothy Stang Josh's hero?

8 Vocabulary

✱ Multi-word verbs (1)

a Look at the examples from the listening.

*Can you **come up** here please?*

*A lot of people wanted to **cut down** the trees.*

Think of other verbs you know that end with *up* or *down*.

b ▶ CD1 T32 Match the sentences with the pictures. Then listen, check and repeat.

1 Climb up!
2 Pick it up, please!
3 Put them on!
4 Get in!
5 Take it off!
6 Come down!
7 Get out!
8 Put it down!

c Look at the verbs in Exercise 8b. Match them with their opposites.

climb up – come down

d Work with a partner. Think of different situations where you can use the verbs in Exercise 8b.

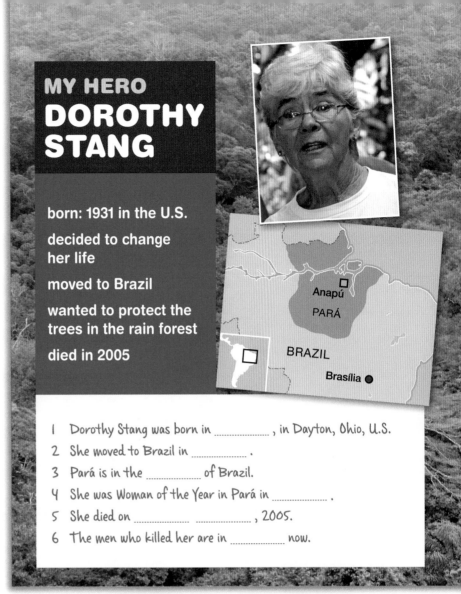

MY HERO
DOROTHY STANG

born: 1931 in the U.S.

decided to change her life

moved to Brazil

wanted to protect the trees in the rain forest

died in 2005

1 Dorothy Stang was born in _____ , in Dayton, Ohio, U.S.
2 She moved to Brazil in _____ .
3 Pará is in the _____ of Brazil.
4 She was Woman of the Year in Pará in _____ .
5 She died on _____ _____ , 2005.
6 The men who killed her are in _____ now.

9 Read and listen

a Look at the photos. Do you know where these things are?

b ▶ CD1 T33 Read the text quickly and listen. Check your ideas.

REMEMBERING HEROES

Countries, cities and people all have their own heroes. There are different kinds of heroes: politicians, soldiers, movie stars, sports stars and musicians. And there are many different ways of remembering them, too. Here are some of the things that we do to make sure that we don't forget our heroes.

• Sometimes we build statues or sculptures of heroes, especially of politicians and soldiers, but sometimes of writers, too. Many cities in South America have a statue of Simón Bolívar. He helped lead many South American countries to independence. And the famous Mount Rushmore in the U.S. remembers four U.S. presidents of the past.

• We often remember soldiers and other people who died in war with a monument, like the Monument to the People's heroes in Beijing, China, or a memorial, like the Eternal Flame at the Tomb of the Unknown Soldier in Paris, France.

• Some countries have a special memorial day, like the one every January in the U.S. for Dr. Martin Luther King Jr., the human rights leader.

• When Lady Diana Spencer died in 1997, in Paris, many people left flowers and messages near the place where the car accident happened. Now there is a Diana, Princess of Wales Memorial Fountain in Hyde Park in London.

• Sometimes places are named after famous people. For example, Liverpool, in England, and Rio de Janeiro, in Brazil, both have airports named after local musicians, John Lennon and Tom Jobim.

• In Hollywood, the Walk of Fame has the names of movie, TV and music celebrities in stars on the sidewalk. Very famous celebrities have their handprints, footprints and autographs in cement at Hollywood's Grauman's Chinese Theatre.

Different countries and people remember their heroes in different ways, including many ways that are not mentioned here. Perhaps in your country there are some different ways. What are they?

c Read the text again and:

1 give four examples of different kinds of heroes.

2 give an example of a statue built to remember a hero.

3 say when Martin Luther King Jr. Day is.

4 give two examples of places named after famous people.

5 say what the Walk of Fame is.

d Work in pairs or groups. Answer the questions.

1 Which of the people in the text did you already know about?

2 What other ways can you think of to remember heroes?

3 How are heroes remembered in your country?

10 Vocabulary

✻ Memory words

Use a word from the box to complete each sentence.

> forget   unforgettable   ~~memories~~   memory
> remember   memorial   forgetful

1 I have a lot of great *memories* of our vacation last year.

2 It was a fantastic day. I'll always _____ it.

3 My brother has an amazing _____ for names and faces.

4 When you finish using the computer, don't _____ to turn it off.

5 There's a new statue in our town. It's a _____ to a famous writer from our country.

6 My friend Zach didn't remember my birthday or his sister's birthday! He's so _____ .

7 We went to Paris last weekend. We had a great time. It was an _____ vacation.

11 Write

a Read the text that Dave wrote about his hero. Match the questions with the paragraphs. Write numbers 1–3 in the boxes.

a What did this person do? ☐

b Why is this person a hero for you? ☐

c Who is your hero? ☐

1 My hero is Helen Thayer. She was the first woman to walk to the magnetic North Pole alone.

2 Helen Thayer was born in New Zealand, and she lived there when she was a girl. Later, she lived in Guatemala for four years and then in the United States. When she was 50, she had a dream. She wanted to walk to the North Pole alone, and she decided to do it. On her journey, Helen didn't have any help. She was completely alone except for her dog, Charlie, a Canadian husky. The journey was very difficult. She walked 555 km in temperatures of −50°C! Once, seven polar bears attacked Helen and Charlie. Charlie saved Helen's life.

3 Helen Thayer is my hero because she had a dream, and she was determined to make it come true. She was always positive, even in very dangerous and difficult situations.

b Think of someone you think is a hero. Write three paragraphs about your hero. Use Dave's example to help you.

12 Speak

Make a poster about your hero. Then give a presentation to the class.

6 Making friends

* Simple past (regular and irregular verbs; questions and short answers)
* Vocabulary: time expressions (past), sports

1 Read and listen

a How many sports do you know in English? What is your favorite sport?

b Read about two athletes at a World Championship in 1971. What nationalities were the two men? What was their sport?

c ▶ CD1 T34 Now read the text again and listen. Put the pictures in the correct order. Write numbers 1–5 in the boxes.

The friendship
that changed the world

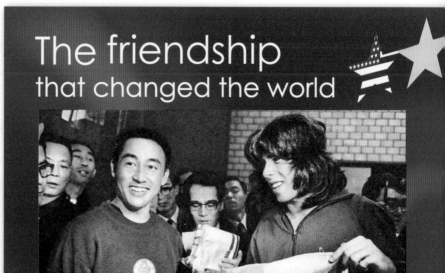

In 1971, the U.S. table tennis team was at the World Championship in Japan. The team from the People's Republic of China was also there. This championship took place during the days of the Cold War. So, the American and the Chinese players didn't even talk to each other.

Glen Cowan, from the U.S. team, didn't like the situation. One day, he saw a Chinese player and invited him to play. They played together for 15 minutes, and Cowan missed the U.S. bus back to the hotel.

Then, something surprising happened. One of the Chinese players waved to Cowan from the Chinese bus. Cowan thought for a moment, and then he got on the bus. But the Chinese players didn't talk to him. Suddenly Zhuang Zedong, three-time world champion, came up to Cowan. "What are you doing?" said the other Chinese players. "Don't talk to him! Don't make trouble!" Zedong gave Cowan a silk scarf. "I give you this to show the friendship of the Chinese people to the American people," he said through a translator. Cowan wanted to give something back, but he didn't have anything with him.

Then the bus arrived at the hotel. There were lots of reporters. It was big news to see an American and a Chinese player together.

Later, Cowan bought a T-shirt with a peace flag on it, and he gave it to Zedong. The two men became friends.

In the same year, the U.S. team got an invitation to visit China, and in February 1972, the U.S. president Richard Nixon went to China on a historic visit. Many people say that the two men and their friendship made a better relationship between their countries possible.

d Answer the questions.

1 Why didn't the American and Chinese players talk to each other?

2 Why did Cowan get on the Chinese team bus?

3 Why didn't Cowan give Zedong a present immediately?

4 Why were there reporters at the hotel when the bus arrived?

e Do you think that Zedong and Cowan stayed friends for a long time? Why / why not?

2 Grammar

✱ Simple past: regular and irregular verbs

a Look at the examples from the text on page 36. How are the verbs in 1 different from the verbs in 2?

1 They **played** for 15 minutes.
He **wanted** to give something back.
The bus **arrived** at the hotel.

2 He **got on** the Chinese bus.
Zedong **gave** him a scarf.
The U.S. president **went** to China.

b Put the verbs from the box in the simple past and write them in the lists. Use the text on page 36 to help you.

~~change~~ ~~see~~ call play miss think get come give want arrive buy become make

Regular verbs	Irregular verbs
changed	*saw*

c Complete the summary. Use the simple past form of the verbs.

There ¹ _was_ (be) a table tennis championship in Japan in 1971. An American and a Chinese player ² _____ (play) together for 15 minutes. The American ³ _____ (miss) his bus, but the Chinese player ⁴ _____ (invite) him onto his bus.

Another Chinese player ⁵ _____ (give) the American a present. The American ⁶ _____ (be) happy, and he ⁷ _____ (want) to give a present back. He ⁸ _____ (buy) a T-shirt for the Chinese player. They ⁹ _____ (become) friends.

In the same year, the American president ¹⁰ _____ (go) to China for a historic visit.

✱ Simple past: questions

d Look at the examples and complete the table.

*Did the Chinese players **talk** to Cowan? No, they **didn't**.*

*Did Cowan and Zedong **become** friends? Yes, they **did**.*

Question	Short answer
_____ I/you/he/she/it/we/they go?	Yes, I/you/he/she/it/we/they _____ .
	No, I/you/he/she/it/we/they _____ (**did not**).

e Put the words in the correct order to make questions.

1 you / go out / last night / did ?

_____

2 music / you / on Sunday / did / listen to ?

_____

3 eggs / you / for breakfast / this morning / eat / did ?

_____

4 you / watch / last night / did / TV ?

_____

5 on vacation / you / last year / did / go ?

_____

3 Speak

Work with a partner. Ask and answer the questions from Exercise 2e.

A: *Did you go out last night?*

B: *No, I didn't. I stayed home and watched TV.*

4 Vocabulary

✱ Time expressions (past)

a When we talk about the past, we can use time expressions like these. Add another example to each list.

> yesterday, yesterday morning, yesterday _____
>
> last night, last week, last April, last _____
>
> an hour ago, four days ago, _____ ago

b Complete the sentences with your own information.

1 Four hours ago, I was _____ _____ .

2 Last night, I went to bed at _____ .

3 Yesterday evening, I _____ _____ .

4 Last Saturday, I _____ _____ .

5 Eight years ago, I was _____ _____ .

6 My last vacation was _____ _____ .

c Complete the sentences. Use a time expression with *ago*.

1 David is 15 now. He started school when he was five.
  David started school *ten years ago* .

2 I met your cousin last Saturday. It's Wednesday today.
  I met your cousin _____ .

3 It's 10:30 now. My English class began at 9:30.
  My English class began _____ .

4 Summer vacation started at the end of June. It's the end of August now.
  Summer vacation started _____ .

5 Speak

Work in small groups. Ask and answer the questions. Use *ago* in your answers.

When / start school?

When / begin learning English?

When / arrive at school this morning?

When / first meet your best friend?

A: *When did you start school?*   B: *Nine years ago.*

6 Vocabulary

✱ Sports

a ▶ CD1 T35 Write the words under the pictures. Then listen, check and repeat.

> ~~cycling~~ basketball hockey skateboarding
> snowboarding surfing swimming volleyball skiing

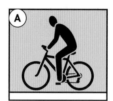
cycling

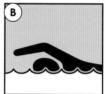
_____

_____

_____

_____

_____

_____

_____

_____

b Work with a partner or in a group. Answer the questions about the sports in Exercise 6a.

Which sports ...

1 are team sports?

2 use equipment with wheels?

3 are water sports?

4 are in the Winter Olympics?

5 are popular in your country?

6 do you do?

7 do you like watching?

7 Pronunciation

▶ CD1 T36 Pronunciation section starts on page 114.

8 Listen

Nick

Dan

Mr. Stern

Mr. Winter

a Look at the pictures of four people in a TV show. Read their names.

b Look at the pictures from the TV show.

A

B
HOME 2 VISITORS 3

C

D
HOME 4 V

E
Stern?
No way!

F

G
OVERS 5

H
1

1 What do you think the relationship is between the four people?

2 ▶ **CD1 T37** Put the pictures in order to tell the story. Then listen and check your ideas.

c Work with a partner. Tell the story to your partner. Use the pictures to help you.

9 Listen: a song

a Read the words of the song. Put the phrases in the box into the correct spaces.

> a little smarter than I am
> I've got them, too
> from your nice warm bed
> We stick together

b ▶ **CD1 T38** Listen and check.

You've got a friend in me
Randy Newman

You've got a friend in me, you've got a friend in me.

When the road looks rough ahead

And you're miles and miles [1] _____

You just remember what your old pal said, boy,

You've got a friend in me.

Yeah, you've got a friend in me.

You've got a friend in me, you've got a friend in me.

If you've got troubles, [2] _____ .

There isn't anything I wouldn't do for you.

[3] _____ we can see it through, 'cos

You've got a friend in me, yeah, you've got a friend in me.

Some other folks might be [4] _____ .

Bigger and stronger, too, baby.

None of them will ever love you the way I do.

It's me and you, boy.

And as the years go by, our friendship will never die.

You're gonna see, it's our destiny.

You've got a friend in me, you've got a friend in me,

Yeah, you've got a friend in me.

Not a nice thing to say

10 ▶ CD1 T39 Read and listen

a Look at the photostory. Who is unhappy? Who is he unhappy with? Read and listen to find the answers.

Alex: So, what should we do after school?

Matt: How about baking cookies for the party on Saturday?

Emily: Sounds good to me.

Alex: Yeah. Everyone can come to my house.

Kim: But don't let Matt bake any cookies!

Matt: Why not?

Kim: Do you remember the time when you made pizza for us? It was horrible!

Matt: It wasn't that bad! And I remember you ate it.

Alex: *Not* a very nice thing to say, Kim.

Kim: Oh, Alex. I was only joking. Can't we make jokes about friends?

Emily: Sure, Kim. But on the other hand, real friends try not to hurt each other's feelings.

Kim: OK. I'm sorry I hurt your feelings, Matt. I didn't mean to.

Matt: Let's just forget about it. So – see you all tomorrow.

Kim: Oh, no. He isn't very happy, is he?

Emily: No, I don't think so. And to be honest, I'm not surprised.

b Complete the sentences with the names: Kim, Matt, Emily or Alex.

1   _Matt_ suggests baking cookies for the party.

2   .... says Matt made an awful pizza one time.

3   .... gets a little angry.

4   .... tells Kim that she wasn't very friendly.

5   .... says it's OK to make jokes about friends.

6   .... says real friends don't hurt each other's feelings.

7   .... says sorry to Matt.

8   .... thinks it's normal that Matt isn't happy.

Everyday English

a Find expressions 1–6 in the photostory. Who says them?

1 How about … ?

2 on the other hand, …

3 I didn't mean to.

4 Let's just forget about it.

5 I don't think so.

6 to be honest, …

b Read the dialogues. Use the expressions in Exercise 11a to complete them.

1 A: Is Hannah German?

B: [1] *I don't think so* . I think she's from Austria.

2 A: [2] _____ going for a walk?

B: Well, I'm a little tired, so [3] _____ , I don't want to go out.

3 A: Mrs. Jones gave us a lot of homework, didn't she?

B: Yes, a lot! But [4] _____ , she didn't give us very much homework last week.

4 A: I'm sorry I broke your camera.
[5] _____

B: [6] _____ . It was an old camera anyway.

Discussion box

1 Matt is hurt when Kim makes a joke about his cooking. How would you react in the same situation?

2 Kim was "only joking." Discuss possible reasons why she was joking.

A: *Maybe Kim likes Matt, and that's why she made the joke.*

B: *I'm not sure. I think she said it because…*

 Improvisation

Work with a partner. Take two minutes to prepare a short role play. Try to use some of the expressions from Exercise 11a. Do not write the text, just agree on your ideas for a short scene. Then act it out.

Roles: Kim and her mom

Situation: At home later the same day

Basic idea: Kim and her mom talk about Matt.

Use one of these sentences to start the conversation:

Kim: Can I ask you something, Mom?

Mom: You don't look very happy today, Kim. Is something wrong?

Reach Out ⊙ DVD Episode 3

a Who are the people in the photo? How does each of them feel, and why, do you think each feels that way?

b Emily, Kim, Alex and Matt have agreed to meet. Suddenly Matt says he can't come. He doesn't give a reason. Work with a partner and write a story (not more than 80 words) to explain why they wanted to meet and what happened.

c Read your stories aloud. Then watch Episode 3 and find out what happened.

14 Write

a Do one of these activities.

- Imagine you are Dan in the story on page 39. Write a diary entry for Dan about what happened.

  Or

- Read Alison's email to her friend, Julia. Answer the questions.

  1 Where did Alison go on the weekend?

  2 What did she do there?

  3 What does she ask Julia to send her?

b Now write a similar email to a friend. Tell him/her about a weekend or day you enjoyed. Use Alison's email to help you.

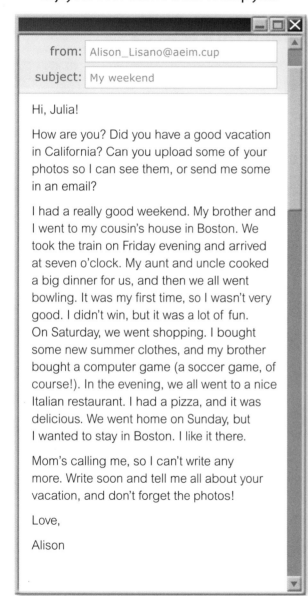

from: Alison_Lisano@aeim.cup

subject: My weekend

Hi, Julia!

How are you? Did you have a good vacation in California? Can you upload some of your photos so I can see them, or send me some in an email?

I had a really good weekend. My brother and I went to my cousin's house in Boston. We took the train on Friday evening and arrived at seven o'clock. My aunt and uncle cooked a big dinner for us, and then we all went bowling. It was my first time, so I wasn't very good. I didn't win, but it was a lot of fun. On Saturday, we went shopping. I bought some new summer clothes, and my brother bought a computer game (a soccer game, of course!). In the evening, we all went to a nice Italian restaurant. I had a pizza, and it was delicious. We went home on Sunday, but I wanted to stay in Boston. I like it there.

Mom's calling me, so I can't write any more. Write soon and tell me all about your vacation, and don't forget the photos!

Love,

Alison

15 Last but not least: more speaking

★ Alibi: a game

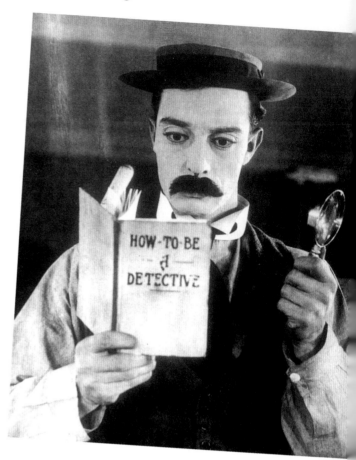

a Two students (A and B) invent a story about what they did last Saturday from 4–7 p.m. The other students cannot hear what they are saying.

b All the other students are detectives. They ask A questions (B can't listen) and take notes. When A doesn't know an answer, he/she has to invent one.

c Now the class asks B questions about what he/she did and tries to find "mistakes" in the alibi.

Class: *Where were you at 6:00 p.m.?*

B: *We were at a football game.*

Class: *Who was with you?*

B: *My friend, Nick.*

Class: *Who played?*

B: *The Bears and the Vikings.*

Class: *Mistake! [A] said the Bears and the Lions. What happened ... ?*

Check your progress

1 Grammar

a Complete the dialogue with the simple past form of *be*.

A: You [1] _____weren't_____ at school yesterday afternoon. Where [2] _____ you?

B: I [3] _____ at home. There [4] _____ a soccer game on television.

A: [5] _____ it a good game?

B: No, it [6] _____ ! Both teams [7] _____ awful! ☐ 6

b Complete the sentences. Use the simple past form of the verbs.

1 In 1950, there _____were_____ (be) 199,854 people at the World Cup Final between Brazil and Uruguay in Rio de Janeiro. They _____ (see) a great game, but Brazil _____ (not win).

2 The Swedish athlete Oskar Gomar Swann _____ (become) famous when he _____ (win) a silver medal in shooting at the Olympic Games in Antwerp in 1920. He _____ (be) 72 years old.

3 At the 1984 Olympic Games in Los Angeles, Carl Lewis _____ (win) four gold medals.

4 In the first round of the long jump, Lewis _____ (jump) 8.54 meters. After that, he _____ (stop). "Nobody can beat me," he _____ (say).

5 I _____ (go) to the movies last night, but I _____ (not enjoy) it very much.

6 A: What _____ Victor _____ (say) to you yesterday?

   B: He _____ (not say) anything!

7 A: _____ you _____ (see) Alyssa last night?

   B: No, I _____ (not see) Alyssa, but I _____ (see) Jamie.

8 A: Where _____ you _____ (go) last summer?

   B: We _____ (go) to New York City, but we _____ (not go) up the Empire State Building. ☐ 19

2 Vocabulary

a Complete the sentences with the words in the box.

up   down   ~~out~~   on   off

1 Let's go _____out_____ tonight. I don't want to stay home.

2 Leo, look at all your books on the floor! Pick them _____ , please.

3 This bag is very heavy. I'm going to put it _____ for a minute.

4 It's cold today. You should put _____ a warm coat.

5 It's hot in here. I'm going to take my sweater _____ . ☐ 4

b Fill in the puzzle with names of sports. What is the mystery word?

	1	s	n	o	w	b	o	a	r	d	i	n	g
2													
				3							
	4									
					p		
	5						
	6						
	7						

1 You do this on a board in snow.

2 You need six players, a ball and a net to play this game.

3 You need a bike for this sport.

4 You do this in a pool.

5 You do this in the mountains in winter.

6 _____ is a winter team game.

7 You go to the ocean with a board for this sport. ☐ 6

How did you do?

Check your score.

Total score	☺	☺	☹
☐ 35	Very good	OK	Not very good
Grammar	25 – 20	19 – 16	15 or less
Vocabulary	10 – 8	7 – 6	5 or less

Successful people

* *have to / don't have to*
* Vocabulary: jobs, work and money

1 Read and listen

a Look at the photos. Match the people with the jobs. Write 1–4 in the boxes.

> 1 athlete   2 actor   3 businessperson   4 TV show host

What does "success" mean?

All the people on this page are "successful" in some way. They're very different people and they do different things, but what they have in common is "success."

But if we say, "This person is successful," what do we really mean? Do we mean that the person is rich? Do we mean that she or he is famous and everybody recognizes them on the street? Or do they have to be very, very good at the things that they do for us to say that they are "successful"?

Some people say that "success" is none of these things. It's just being happy, and it doesn't matter if you are rich or famous or not. After all, there are a lot of "successful" people who aren't very happy, and lots of happy people who aren't "successful."

What do you think?

Jeff Bezos

Wealthy creator of Amazon.com

Ana Ivanovic

Number 1 women's tennis player in 2008

Oprah Winfrey

People (even politicians) listen to her.

Johnny Depp

A famous face in many movies

e ▶ **CD1 T40** Listen to six teenagers talking about success. Which things in Exercise 1d does each one talk about?

Speaker 1 ....

Speaker 2 ....

Speaker 3 ....

Speaker 4 ....

Speaker 5 ....

Speaker 6 ....

f Think of someone you know who is successful but not famous. In what ways is this person successful? Discuss your ideas with a partner.

b In what ways are the people above different? In what ways are they similar?

c Read the text quickly. Find three things that can mean "success."

d What do you think success means? Check (✓) the things that you think are necessary for someone to be "successful." Then compare your ideas with a partner.

a being famous ☐

b being happy ☐

c having a lot of money ☐

d being respected ☐

e being intelligent ☐

f doing what you want to do ☐

g being good at what you do ☐

h enjoying your life ☐

2 Grammar

✱ *have to / don't have to*

a Look at the examples from the reading and listening texts. Complete the rule and the table.

You **have to** be good at what you do.   You **don't have to** be famous to be successful.
You **don't have to** be intelligent.   You **have to** enjoy your work.

Affirmative	Negative	Question	Short answer
I/you/we/they **have to** go	I/you/we/they _____ **(do not) have to** go	_____ I/you/we/they **have to** go?	Yes, I/you/we/they _____ . No, I/you/we/they _____ **(do not)**.
he/she/it _____ go	he/she/it _____ **(does not) have to** go	_____ he/she/it **have to** go?	Yes, he/she/it _____ . No, he/she/it _____ **(does not)**.

RULE:

We use _____ to say "This is necessary."

We use _____ to say "This isn't necessary."

b Complete the sentences. Use *have/has to* or *don't/doesn't have to*.

1 If you want to work in the U.S., you ___*have to*___ speak good English.

2 My sister has a young baby, so she often _____ get up during the night.

3 My friend gets good test scores, but he _____ work very hard. In fact, he never studies before a test.

4 Tomorrow is Sunday, so I _____ go to school. Great!

5 At our school, we _____ wear a uniform. It's dark blue with a white shirt.

6 At my cousins' school, they _____ wear a uniform. They can wear what they want.

3 Pronunciation

▶ **CD1 T41** Pronunciation section starts on page 114.

4 Speak

a Write ✓ for the things you have to do at home. Write ✗ for the things you don't have to do.

get up at the same time on the weekend as on weekdays

do homework

do housework

cook

do yard work

take care of (pets / brothers and sisters)

b Work with a partner. Ask and answer questions about the activities in Exercise 4a.

A: *On the weekend, do you have to get up at the same time as on weekdays?*

B: *No, I don't. But I can't stay in bed all day! What about you?*

A: *I can get up later, but I have to do yard work on Sundays.*

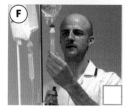

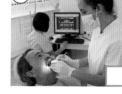

5 Vocabulary

✱ Jobs

a ▶ **CD1 T42** Match the names of the jobs with the pictures above. Write 1–12 in the boxes. Then listen, check and repeat.

> 1 engineer   2 sales clerk   3 nurse
> 4 vet   5 doctor   6 flight attendant
> 7 lawyer   8 ~~pilot~~   9 dentist
> 10 firefighter   11 teacher   12 architect

b Write the names of three more jobs you are interested in. Use a dictionary or ask your teacher.

1 _____
2 _____
3 _____

LOOK!

When we talk about jobs in English, we often use *a/an* before the job:
*My mother's **a** nurse.*
*I want to be **an** engineer when I leave school.*

c ▶ **CD1 T43** Listen to four teenagers. Which job does each one want to do in the future? Fill in the blanks with four of the jobs in the box.

> pilot   singer   doctor
> teacher   tennis player   vet
> computer programmer   flight attendant

1 Luke: _____
2 Mia: _____
3 Sam: _____
4 Jodi: _____

6 Speak

a ▶ **CD1 T44** Read the dialogue between two students. Fill in the blanks with the phrases from the box. Then listen and check your answers.

> speak English   be a pilot   not sure
> get good grades   finish school
> I'd like   math and physics   have to do

Linda: What do you want to be when you
 1 _____ ?

Julio: I want to 2 _____ .

Linda: Really? What do you 3 _____ for that?

Julio: You have to 4 _____ , and you have to be good at 5 _____ . And you have to 6 _____ really well. What about you? What do you want to do?

Linda: I'm 7 _____ , but I think
 8 _____ to be a vet.

b Work with a partner. Continue the dialogue between Linda and Julio. Use the phrases in the box. Then practice the whole dialogue.

> like animals   study for five years
> get good grades   be good at biology

c Work with a different partner. Find out what he/she wants to be. Use the dialogue between Linda and Julio to help you.

7 Read

a Look at the photos. Answer the questions.

1 Do you know who the person is?

2 What is the sport?

3 Why do you think the text has the title *Racing to Success*?

Read the text quickly and check your ideas.

b Read the text again. Answer the questions.

1 Where does Joey Logano live?

2 When did he start competing in races?

3 How old was he when he set a record at the Atlanta Motor Speedway?

4 What did Mark Martin say about him?

5 When did Logano start racing with NASCAR?

6 How old was he when he won the Nationwide Series?

c What do you know about Joey Logano since 2009? Tell the class.

d Work in groups. Make a list of three people who became famous when they were young. Makes notes about each of them. Then tell the others in the class about them and why you chose them.

RACING TO SUCCESS

Start your engines! The race begins . . . Joey Logano is a young man with a big career.

Joey was born in 1990 in Connecticut and now lives in North Carolina in the United States. When Joey was six, he started racing small cars in competitions. He began to win many races, but they weren't big races. His parents decided to move to Atlanta, Georgia, so Joey could compete in bigger and better competitions. When he was 12, he set a record by winning 14 races in a row at the Atlanta Motor Speedway. He continued to win many races, and eventually began racing with regular-sized race cars.

When Joey was 15 years old, he met the race car driver Mark Martin. Martin is a famous NASCAR driver. NASCAR is the National Association for Stock Car Auto Racing, and it is the biggest and most popular car-racing organization in the United States. Martin was enthusiastic about Joey and thought he was "the real deal." He said, "I am absolutely, 100-percent positive, without a doubt that he can be one of the greatest that ever raced in NASCAR. I'm positive. There's no doubt in mind."

Martin was right. Joey started as a NASCAR driver in 2007. NASCAR has many races, and at first, Joey was only able to compete in smaller races because of his age. In his first NASCAR season, he won a championship. In 2008, he was able to compete in bigger NASCAR competitions. He competed in one of the top NASCAR racing series called the Nationwide Series, and at 18, he became the youngest winner in Nationwide Series history.

In 2009, he became the youngest winner in another top NASCAR racing series called the Sprint Cup Series, and he also won the Nationwide Series for the fifth time. To be one of the best drivers in the history of racing, Joey has to win many more races. But at 19, he's off to a good start.

Culture in mind

Read and listen

a Match the words in the box with the photos and captions. Write 1–5 in the boxes.

1 mowing lawns 2 delivering newspapers 3 babysitting 4 dog walking 5 working online

b ▶ CD1 T43 What do the five things have in common? Read the text quickly and check your ideas.

c Which job (or jobs) above involves:

1   a computer? 4   carrying things?
2   walking?   5   going to another person's house?
3   a bicycle?   6   animals?

d Put the five jobs in the text in order. 1 = the job you would like to do most, 5 = the job you would like to do least. Compare with a partner.

Teenagers Earning Money

In the United States, you can only get a full-time job if you are 16 years old or older. But there are things that teenagers can do to earn some spending money. Here are a few ideas.

Parents with young children sometimes want to go out for dinner or to the movies, but they don't want to leave their children alone. So, they ask a teenager to stay in the house and look after their children while they are out. If the children take naps or go to bed early, you can do some of your homework!

Teenagers can deliver newspapers. You usually ride a bike around a neighborhood and leave a newspaper at each house. Normally you have to have your own bike. You have to get up early, too, because people want to read their newspapers with their breakfast!

Some adults have a dog, but they don't have time to take it for a walk. Dogs need a lot of exercise! So some teenagers work as dog walkers. It's a good idea—you earn money and you're outside in the fresh air. You get some exercise, too!

Teenagers can work at home on their computers. Some companies pay teens to take online surveys. They want to know what teens are interested in. It's a fun and easy way to make money. You can also design web pages for friends or adults. Do you have any old toys, books or CDs you don't use? Sell them online and make some money!

9 Vocabulary

✻ Work and money

a Complete each sentence with a word from the box.

> Saturday job   earn   full-time   ~~part-time~~
> spending money   save   spend   waste

1 She only works two hours every morning. It's just a __part-time__ job.

2 When I have some money, I always put it in the bank and _____ it.

3 I work every Saturday to _____ some money for myself.

4 I go to bed early on Fridays because I've got a _____ .

5 I like to _____ my money on clothes and CDs.

6 I don't work at all because my parents give me _____ every month.

7 That movie is really awful, so don't _____ your money by going to see it!

8 My brother works 9–5, five days a week. It's a _____ job!

b What's the difference between:

1 a part-time job and a full-time job?

2 to earn money and to spend money?

3 to spend money and to save money?

4 to spend money and to waste money?

1

Sometimes adults pay teenagers to mow their lawns. It's a great job because you get fresh air and exercise. Mow a lawn carefully and people will want you to do it again. Then you have regular customers, because grass always grows!

These are all great ideas. You can choose one of them to earn some money. Then you can spend it or save it! But don't forget it's important to always tell an adult where you're going. Be safe when you work!

10 Speak

a Choose a job that you want to do when you finish school.

b List the good things about this job, and some "not-so-good" things, too, and think about why you want to have this job.

c Talk for about half a minute about the job.

11 Write

a Read the questions Hakan asked his uncle. Then read what he wrote about his uncle's job. Match the questions with the paragraphs. Write 1–3 in the boxes.

a What do you like and dislike about your job? ☐

b Why did you decide to be a dentist, and what did you have to do to get the job? ☐

c What do you have to do in your job? ☐

1 When he was young, my uncle Erol always wanted to be a policeman, but when he was 18, he decided to be a dentist because dentists earn more money. To be a dentist, he had to study hard for five years at a university and take a lot of exams.

2 In his job, my uncle has to clean and fix people's teeth, and sometimes he has to pull them out! He doesn't have to get up very early, but he has to work hard, usually from 10:00 in the morning to 7:30 in the evening from Monday to Saturday. It's a full-time job.

3 He likes his job because he never has to take his work home, and he meets lots of people. One thing he doesn't like is that he can't really talk to his patients because he is working inside their mouths!

b Ask a friend or family member about his/her job. Then write about it using the information you get. Use Hakan's questions and text to help you.

For your portfolio

8 Eat for life.

* Count and noncount nouns
* *a/an* and *some*; *much* and *many*; *some* and *any*
* Vocabulary: food and drink

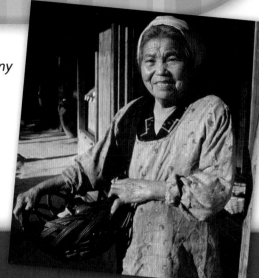

1 Read and listen

a Think of things that can help people live a long time and compare with a partner. Then read the text quickly and check your ideas.

A long and healthy life

Everyone wants to be healthy and live a long time. But how can we do it? Some years ago, a 90-year-old American writer gave some advice for a long and healthy life:

* Believe in yourself.
* Keep your mind active.
* Be positive.
* Love people and enjoy helping others.

The women of Okinawa, in Japan, are another great example. They live a long time, they are very fit and they don't have many diseases or heart problems. Their secret? They exercise every day, they don't have much stress in their lives, and, in general, they are positive and active.

But of course, diet is important, too. The Okinawa women eat tofu, fish, green vegetables, carrots, fruit and sweet potatoes. They eat some meat, but they don't eat any fat from the meat. And they eat seaweed. This contains many different vitamins and minerals and is good for your heart.

The Mediterranean diet is very healthy, too. It consists of vegetables, tomatoes, lemons, fish, beans, garlic, cheese, yogurt, rice and pasta. The fat in this diet is "good fat." It comes from olive oil and from fish.

So, what do these two diets tell us?

* Don't eat any bad fats – like fats in sweets, fried food and meat.
* Eat healthy carbohydrates – vegetables, fruit, potatoes, rice.
* Don't use much oil when cooking. If you use oil, use a good one like olive oil. And avoid deep-fried food!
* If you're a little hungry, eat an apple or a carrot – not a bag of potato chips!

Eat well, live an active and stress-free life, and you'll live a long time.

b ▶ CD1 T46 Now read the text again and listen. Answer the questions.

1 Does the American writer give advice for your mind or your body?
2 Why do the women in Okinawa live a long time?
3 Why is seaweed good for you?
4 Where does the fat come from in the Mediterranean diet?

c Do you know any people who are very old? Tell the class about them. Talk about their lifestyle and diet.

2 Vocabulary

✳ Food and drink

▶ **CD1 T47** Write the words under the pictures. Then listen, check and repeat.

apples   carrots   eggs   meat   fruit
bread   ~~vegetables~~   tomatoes   orange juice
beans   onions   sugar   mineral water   rice

A   B   C   D   E   F   G

vegetables   ____   ____   ____   ____   ____   ____

H   I   J   K   L   M   N

____   ____   ____   ____   ____   ____   ____

3 Grammar

✳ Count and noncount nouns

a Read the rule. Then underline the count nouns and (circle) the noncount nouns in examples 1–4.

> **RULE:** In English, we can count some nouns: *one apple, two bananas, three carrots*, etc. We call these words *count nouns*.
>
> There are some nouns we can't count, for example: *food* and *fruit*. These nouns have no plural. We call them *noncount nouns*.

1   Eat an <u>apple</u> or a <u>carrot</u>.
2   They do some exercise every day.
3   Some years ago …
4   The Okinawa women eat fish and green vegetables.

b Complete the lists with words from Exercise 2.

Count nouns	Noncount nouns
vegetables	fruit

✳ *a/an* and *some*

c Look again at the examples in Exercise 3a. Complete the rule with *count* or *noncount*.

> **RULE:** We use *a/an* with singular ____ nouns. We use *some* with plural ____ nouns. We use *some* with ____ nouns.

d Complete the sentences with *a, an* or *some*.

1   I'd like __some__ sugar in my coffee.
2   I'm going to the store. Mom needs ____ meat and ____ eggs.
3   This is ____ beautiful apple!
4   ____ onion is ____ vegetable.
5   Have ____ fruit. There are ____ nice bananas in the kitchen.
6   She needs ____ bread, ____ cheese and ____ tomato to make a sandwich.
7   I'm a little hungry. I think I'll eat ____ orange.

✱ *much* and *many*

e Look at the examples. Then complete the rule.

*Don't use **much** oil.*

*They don't have **many diseases** or **heart problems**.*

*How **many meals** do you eat a day?*

*How **much water** do you drink?*

> **RULE:** We can use *much* and *many* in negative sentences and questions. We use *many* with plural _____ nouns. We use *much* with _____ nouns.

f (Circle) the correct words in questions 1–6. Then match the questions with the answers.

1 Is there (much) / many milk in the fridge?
2 How *much* / *many* potatoes do you want?
3 How *much* / *many* time do we have?
4 Are there *much* / *many* people in the café?
5 How *much* / *many* subjects do you study?
6 How *much* / *many* money do you have?

a Yes, there are about 50.
b $15.
c No, there isn't.
d Two, please.
e Ten minutes.
f Seven.

4 Speak

a Work with a partner. Discuss the quiz questions and choose the answers you think are correct.

b Ask your partner about the things in the quiz. For example:

Do you eat a lot of hamburgers?

How many hamburgers do you eat every month?

How often do you eat an apple?

1 How many calories are there in an average hamburger?
A 150　　B 220　　C 280

2 How many calories are there in an apple?
A 80　　B 100　　C 120

3 How many calories do you burn if you swim for 20 minutes?
A 60　　B 90　　C 140

4 How many calories do you burn if you run for 20 minutes?
A 200　　B 300　　C 400

5 How much water should people drink every day?
A three glasses　B eight glasses　C ten to twelve glasses

6 How much sleep does an average person get every night?
A 7 hours　　B 8.5 hours　　C 9.5 hours

5 Pronunciation

▶ **CD1 T48 and T49** Pronunciation section starts on page 114.

6 Listen

a ▶ **CD1 T50** Match the dishes on the school cafeteria menu with the pictures. Write the numbers 1–10. Then listen and check.

Ⓐ  4

Ⓑ

Ⓒ

Ⓓ

Ⓔ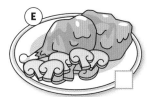

Ⓕ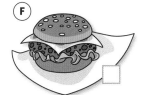

Ⓖ

Ⓗ

Ⓘ

Ⓙ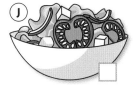

Appetizers
1 Pasta (with tomato sauce)
2 Vegetable soup Ⓥ
3 Tossed salad

Main courses
(with vegetables or French fries)
4 Fish
5 Chicken and mushrooms
6 Cheeseburger
7 Vegetarian curry and rice Ⓥ

Desserts
8 Yogurt (various fruit flavors)
9 Ice cream
10 Cheese

b ▶ **CD1 T51** Listen to the dialogue at the school cafeteria. Write down what Annie and Jack ask for.

1 Annie: _____

2 Jack: _____

7 Grammar

✶ *some* and *any*

a Look at the examples from the dialogue. Complete the rule.

*I'd like **some yogurt**, please.*
*I'd like **some carrots**.*
*We don't have **any carrots** today.*
*Do you want **any dessert**?*

> **RULE:** With noncount and plural nouns, we usually use _____ in affirmative sentences, and we usually use _____ in negative sentences and questions.

b Complete the sentences with *some* or *any*.

1 I wanted to buy ___*some*___ food, but I didn't have _____ money.

2 A: Do we have _____ homework tonight?
   B: Yes, we have _____ grammar exercises to do.

3 Mario bought _____ new socks last week, but he didn't buy _____ shoes.

4 A: Let's listen to _____ music.
   B: OK. Did you bring _____ CDs?

5 I'd like to make _____ sandwiches. The problem is I have _____ cheese, but I don't have _____ butter.

8 Speak

a In Exercise 6b, who orders a healthy lunch, Annie or Jack? Discuss in a small group.

b Work with a partner. One of you works in the cafeteria. The other one orders a meal. Then change roles.

Look at the menu in Exercise 6a. Choose what to order.

Use these expressions to help you.

What would you like?	*Can I have ...... ?*
What else?	*I'd like ......, please.*
Here you are.	*Thanks!*

Two scoops of ice cream

9 ▶ **CD1 T52** **Read and listen**

a Look at the photostory. Who do you think orders a double ice cream, Emily or Matt? Read and listen to find the answer.

Matt: I really like coming here. It's nice after a long day at school.

Emily: Yeah. And today was a long day. That class this afternoon with Mr. Jackson ... wow!

Matt: Didn't you like it?

Emily: It was OK. But, I mean ... how many classes are we going to have about food and diet and stuff?

Matt: Yeah, I know what you mean. It's important though.

Emily: Sure, of course it is. But then I look at the desserts on the menu and ...

Matt: And?

Emily: And there's this little voice inside my head. It's saying, "Bad, bad!" And it sounds like Mr. Jackson!

Matt: Yeah, I know that voice.

Emily: I try not to listen to it, but it isn't easy!

Matt: No problem! Just order two scoops of ice cream with chocolate sauce.

Emily: Are you serious?

Matt: Absolutely! Look, I know a good diet is important. But you have to enjoy life as well.

Emily: That's true. But two scoops of ice cream with chocolate sauce? Isn't that a little too much?

Matt: Well, yes. That's why I can only do this a couple of times a month!

Emily: OK, I'll have the same thing, too!

b Mark the statements *T* (true) or *F* (false).

1 Emily and Matt are at the café after school. $\boxed{T}$

2 They learned about food and diet in class today. ☐

3 Emily thinks they have too many classes about food. ☐

4 Mr. Jackson says, "Bad, bad!" when Emily looks at the menu. ☐

5 Matt has a problem with ice cream with chocolate sauce. ☐

6 Matt is not serious when he says you have to enjoy life. ☐

7 Matt only orders ice cream with chocolate sauce once a month. ☐

10 Everyday English

a Find expressions 1–6 in the photostory. Who says them? Match them with the expressions a–f.

1 ... and stuff. [c]

2 I know what you mean. ☐

3 No problem! ☐

4 Absolutely! ☐

5 ... as well. ☐

6 ... a couple of ... ☐

a Yes!

b ... too.

c ... and things like that.

d ... two ...

e Don't worry.

f I understand you.

b Read the dialogue. Use the expressions in Exercise 10a to complete it.

Paula: I'm really tired. Too much work!

Julian: [1] *I know what you mean* .
I did three hours of homework last night. French, math
[2] _____ .

Paula: Me too. But I watched soccer on TV [3] _____ .

Julian: Really? So you did your homework after the game? How did you stay awake?

Paula: [4] _____ !
I just drank [5] _____ cups of coffee.

Julian: So, coffee keeps you awake?

Paula: [6] _____ !
I didn't go to sleep for hours. I'm really tired today, though!

Discussion box

1 Matt says "you have to enjoy life as well." What do you think?

2 How do you relax after a long day at school?

11 Improvisation

Work in groups of three. Take two minutes to prepare a short role play. Try to use some of the expressions from Exercise 10a. Do not write the text, just agree on your ideas for a short scene. Then act it out.

Roles: Matt, Emily and Mr. Jackson

Situation: At the café, a few minutes later

Basic idea: Matt and Emily have just ordered their ice cream. Mr. Jackson comes into the café.

Use one of these sentences to start the conversation:

Mr. Jackson: Emily? Matt? What a surprise to see you here!

Matt: Hello, Mr. Jackson. Would you like to join us?

12 Reach Out DVD Episode 4

a How well do you know Emily, Kim, Matt and Alex? Fill in the blanks with their names.

b Watch Episode 4 and check if you were right.

_____ doesn't like doing yard work.

_____ says _____ eats unhealthily.

_____ thinks he/she isn't overweight.

_____ says that what _____ eats is gross.

_____ wants _____ and _____ to stop arguing.

_____ is worried that the group won't work as a team at the senior center.

_____ didn't mean to be rude.

For your portfolio

13 Write

Write a paragraph about *one* of your partners. Use your notes from Exercise 12 to guide you. Here is an example.

Carol eats three meals a day. She eats a lot of salad and vegetables, but not much meat. She hates carrots! She doesn't eat a lot of snacks, but she sometimes has ice cream or some chocolate. She drinks about eight glasses of water a day.

Carol thinks it's important to stay fit. She plays basketball once a week. She swims and rides her bike, too, and she enjoys going for walks on the weekend.

14 Last but not least: more speaking

a Read the following questions. Take three minutes to think about your answers. Make notes.

1 Which is your favorite eating place (a restaurant, a fast-food place, your grandma's)? What do you especially like about the place and why (the food, the people)?

2 Imagine you have your own restaurant. What is it like?
- What kind of food and drink do you serve?
- Where is it?
- What is the style like?
- Who are the people working there?
- What does it look like?

3 Imagine you are in a restaurant with a famous person.
- Who is the person?
- Where is the restaurant?
- What are you talking about?

b Ask and answer the questions with three other people in your class.

c Share your favorite ideas with the class.

Check your progress

1 Grammar

a Complete the sentences. Use *have/has to* or *don't/doesn't have to.*

1 You _____*have to*_____ understand! There is no way I can accept this.

2 If you want to go to college, you _____ study hard.

3 She _____ buy a computer. She can use my laptop.

4 Students at most schools in England _____ wear a uniform.

5 I understand what you said. You _____ tell me again!

6 Sergio wants to be healthy. He _____ be careful about what he eats.

7 You _____ help me with my work. I can do it by myself. ☐ 6

b (Circle) the correct words.

1 She's buying *a* / (*some*) fruit at the supermarket.

2 Can I have *a* / *an* orange, please?

3 I can't buy it. I don't have *much* / *many* money.

4 How *much* / *many* tomatoes do we have?

5 *Much* / *Many* people live in this city.

6 If you want something to eat, have *a* / *some* sandwich.

7 We have *a* / *some* eggs, but we don't have *much* / *many* bread.

8 We don't have *some* / *any* apples today. Would you like *some* / *any* carrots?

9 Our teacher never gives us *some* / *any* homework before the weekend. She's great! ☐ 8

2 Vocabulary

a Fill in the puzzle with words for food and drink. What's the mystery word?

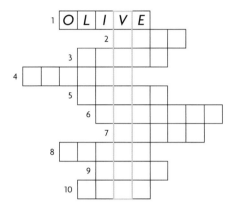

1 _____*Olive*_____ oil is a good oil to use when cooking.

2 They come from chickens and you can fry them or boil them.

3 A lot of people put this in coffee.

4 A lot of people drink _____ juice for breakfast.

5 I'd like a glass of mineral _____ .

6 They are orange and they grow in the ground.

7 You need _____ to make toast.

8 A round fruit that is usually red or green.

9 Chicken, lamb and beef, for example.

10 Food that we get from the ocean. ☐ 9

b Put the letters in order to find the names of jobs.

1	cathree	_____*teacher*_____	5 lpito	_____
2	tindest	_____	6 wrayel	_____
3	crodot	_____	7 rigefhetifr	_____
4	serun	_____	8 eerening	_____

☐ 7

How did you do?

Check your score.

Total score	☺ Very good	☺ OK	☹ Not very good
☐ 30			
Grammar	14 – 11	10 – 9	8 or less
Vocabulary	16 – 13	12 –10	9 or less

9 Learning languages

* Comparatives and superlatives
* Vocabulary: language learning

1 Read and listen

a Look at the pictures and the title of the text. What do you think the text is about? Read the text quickly and check.

b ▶ CD2 T02 Read the text again and listen. Write *T* (true) or *F* (false).

1 Mezzofanti spoke over 38 languages.

2 He traveled to other countries.

3 For Mezzofanti, Arabic was harder to learn than Chinese.

4 One story says that he learned a language in one night.

5 He never met anyone who spoke Old English.

c Do many people in your country speak more than one language? Which languages do people speak?

d One language in the world has more speakers than English. Which do you think it is?

Arabic   Chinese
Russian   Spanish

Speaking in many tongues

Giuseppe Mezzofanti (1774 – 1849) was an Italian cardinal who was perhaps the best language learner ever. He spoke more than 38 languages fluently. He never left Italy, but he learned to speak these languages without an accent. People from all over the world came to talk to him in their native language. All of them were amazed at his fluency.

At the age of 12, Mezzofanti spoke his native Italian, as well as German, Greek, Latin, and at least five other languages. Then he learned Arabic, Russian, Hindi, Old English and Maltese. He also learned Chinese. This was the hardest language for him to learn. It took him four months.

Some stories say he also spoke 30 other languages fairly well and that he could understand another 20 (for example, Tibetan and Icelandic).

Another story says that he heard there were two foreigners in a prison in Rome. So he learned their language in one night and spoke to them the next morning!

It's hard to know if all these stories are true. Some people, for example, ask, "How did he learn Old English without meeting anyone who spoke it?" or "Did he really learn a language in a few weeks – or in one night?" We don't know for sure, but we can say for certain that Giuseppe Mezzofanti became a language-learning legend.

2 Listen

a ► **CD2 T03** Alessandro and Paula are talking about the languages they are learning. Listen and read.

b ► **CD2 T03** Listen again and write the names of the languages.

ALESSANDRO (from Italy)
Native language: Italian
Learning: Spanish, German

ALESSANDRO:
My ¹ _____ is good. It's better than my ² _____ . Of course, for me ³ _____ is easier than ⁴ _____ . That's because it has a lot of words that are almost the same as ⁵ _____ . The grammar is very similar, too.

PAULA (from Argentina)
Native language: Spanish
Learning: English, Portuguese

PAULA:
⁶ _____ pronunciation is difficult for me. But of course ⁷ _____ pronunciation is more difficult! I never know how to pronounce a new word, because the writing and the pronunciation are often very different.

3 Grammar

✳ Comparative adjectives

a  examples of comparisons in the texts in Exercise 2. Then complete the table.

	Adjectives	Comparative form
short adjectives (one syllable)	long short big	long**er** *shorter* bigg**er**
adjectives ending in -y	easy happy	_____ than ... happ**i**er
longer adjectives (two or more syllables)	difficult important	_____ **more** important
irregular adjectives	bad good far	worse _____ farther

b Complete the sentences. Choose the correct adjective and use the comparative form.

1 Italian is *more modern than* (old / modern) Latin.
2 The Amazon River is _____ (short / long) the Mississippi.
3 Iceland is _____ (big / small) India.
4 For most Europeans, learning Chinese is _____ (easy / difficult) learning Italian.
5 Sydney is _____ (close to / far from) my country _____ Paris.

4 Pronunciation

► **CD2 T04** Pronunciation section starts on page 114.

5 Speak

Work with a partner. Compare the things in the list. Use adjectives from the box or other adjectives that you know.

interesting   good
beautiful   exciting
friendly   clean   nice
intelligent   easy
important   quiet   boring

● movies / books
● summer / winter
● soccer / tennis
● dogs / cats
● cities / villages
● Spanish / German

6 Listen

a ▶ **CD2 T05** Listen to the interview with Professor Crystal. <u>Underline</u> the correct answers.

1 The language with the most words is probably English / Chinese / Arabic.

2 Every year, about 250 / 2,500 / 25,000 new words come into English.

3 English has under 1 million / 1 million / more than 1 million words.

4 The most frequent letter in English is *a / e / i*.

5 There are 5 / 10 / 12 meanings for "X" in Professor Crystal's book.

b ▶ **CD2 T05** Listen again. Answer the questions.

1 How many English words do the two biggest dictionaries list?

2 How many words does a native speaker of English usually have in their active vocabulary?

3 How can a woman who speaks Japanese say yes when a man asks her to marry him?

4 How can a woman who speaks Igbo say yes when a man asks her to marry him?

Professor David Crystal is one of the world's most famous experts on language. He is the author of more than 100 books and gives talks all over the world. Two of his most important books are *The Cambridge Encyclopedia of the English Language* and *The Cambridge Encyclopedia of Language*.

7 Vocabulary

✱ Language learning

a Check that you understand these words about learning and speaking languages.

> make mistakes   imitate   corrects   translate   look up
> ~~have an accent~~   means   guess   communicate

b ▶ **CD2 T06** Read the text. Fill in the blanks with the words and phrases from Exercise 7a. Then listen and check.

Advice for language learners

" It can sometimes be difficult to learn a foreign language fluently. But there are many things you can do to make your learning more successful.

When you speak a foreign language, it's normal to [1] *have an accent* . That's OK – other people can usually understand. It's a good idea to listen to CDs and try to [2] _____ other speakers to make your pronunciation better.

If you see a new word, and you don't know what it [3] _____ , you can sometimes

[4] _____ the meaning from words you know, or you can [5] _____ the word in a dictionary.

A lot of good language learners try not to [6] _____ things from their first language. Translation is sometimes a good idea, but try to think in the foreign language if you can!

It's also normal to [7] _____ . When your teacher [8] _____ a mistake in your writing or speaking, think about it and try to see why it's wrong. But it's more important to [9] _____ , so don't be afraid to speak! "

a Read the sentences on the cards. Two of them are not true. Which do you think they are?

The longest word in the English language is *dispercombobulation* – it has 19 letters.

The most frequent letter in English is *e*. The least frequent is *q*.

The easiest language to learn in the world is Portoni, a language spoken in Papua New Guinea. It doesn't have any grammar, and there are only about 1,750 words in the language.

AMAZING FACTS — OR JUST LIES??

The shortest place names only have one letter. There are towns in Norway and Sweden called Å and there is a river in Oregon, in the U.S., called D.

There are 820 languages in Papua New Guinea, 742 in Indonesia and 516 in Nigeria. South Africa has the most official languages in the world.

Somalia is the only African country where everybody speaks the same language (Somali).

The longest one-word place name in the world is in New Zealand: *Taumatawhakatangihangakoauauotamateaturipukakapikimaungahoronukupokaiwhenuakitanatahu.*

b Cover the text. Can you answer these questions?

1 Which country has the most official languages?
2 What is the most frequent letter in English?
3 In which African country does everyone speak the same language?
4 Which letter is the name of a river in the U.S.?

c Look at the table. Write the adjectives from the box in the second column. Then fill in the comparative and superlative forms.

difficult big happy fantastic important

	Adjectives	Comparative form	Superlative form
short adjectives (one syllable)	long short small	longer shorter	the longest ....
short adjectives ending in one vowel + one consonant	.... fat	fatter	the fattest
adjectives ending in -y	easy	easier	....
longer adjectives (two or more syllables)	frequent	more frequent	the most frequent ....
irregular adjectives	bad good many	worse better more	....

d Complete the sentences. Use the superlative form of the adjectives.

1 Many people say that Hungarian is one of *the most difficult* (difficult) languages.

2 When Sarah won $1,000, she was the .... (happy) woman in the world.

3 The Internet was one of .... (important) inventions of the 1960s.

4 Vatican City is .... (small) country in the world.

5 When my grandmother died, it was one of .... (bad) times in my life.

6 The Amazon is .... (long) river in the world.

Culture in mind

9 Read and listen

a Think of three words in your own language that teenagers often say and adults don't say.

b Think of three words in your own language that teachers or parents say a lot and you never say.

c Share your ideas with a partner.

d ▶ CD2 T07 Read the text and check your ideas.

Teen talk

It's 2010, outside of a school somewhere in the U.S. Some teenagers are talking. One says to another, "I'm tired of chillaxing after school. We do this 24/7. Let's go get some eats."

Two adults are walking by. They hear what the teenagers are saying, but they don't understand a word. (What the teenager said was, "I'm tired of hanging around after school. We do this all the time. Let's go get some food.")

This is nothing new. Teenagers always invent new words and phrases. They create words for everyday things, words that mean *good* or *parents* or *bad* or *good-looking*, and so on. Look at these different ways of saying *good* in recent decades:

> 1960s – groovy
> *1970s – fab*
> 1980s – wicked
> 1990s – sweet
> 2000s – tight

But, of course, the words you use depend on your interests, your friends, the music you listen to and the part of the country you live in. Different groups of teenagers have different likes and dislikes, and so they also have different expressions.

So why do teenagers invent new words, or invent new meanings for old words? Many people think it's because they don't want adults to understand, but that probably isn't true. The real reason is that teenagers want to feel that they're part of a group that speaks the same language, a language that is different from the one their parents and other adults speak. And also teenagers like to be creative and play with language, so they have fun creating new words.

And what do the *rents* (parents) think about it all? Most of them don't worry about it. After all, they had their own special words when they were teenagers, too. But, some adults complain about "teen talk" and get very annoyed by it. But that's all part of the fun for the teenagers!

e Match the words with their definitions.

1 walk by   *f*
2 hang around
3 invent
4 decades
5 expression
6 complain

a to wait or spend time somewhere
b groups of ten years
c a word or a phrase
d to create something new
e to say that something isn't (or wasn't) good
f go by without stopping

f Complete the sentences with words from Exercise 9e. Use the correct form when necessary.

1 *Decades* ago, many of the words we use now didn't exist.
2 When I was a child, I loved _____ new words.
3 Some of my friends _____ for hours after school.
4 What does this _____ mean?
5 She _____ to her math teacher that she had too much homework.
6 Ismahan _____ Jordan's house on her way to school.

10 Write

Do one of these activities.

a Write about the languages you speak. Use the texts by Alessandro and Paula on page 59 to help you.

b Imagine you are taking an English class at a language school in Britain or the U.S. Write an email to an English-speaking friend. Think about these questions.

- Where are you writing from? (London, New York, Miami?)
- Do you like the English class? What kind of things are you doing in class?
- Who is your teacher?
- How many students are in your class? Where are they from?
- Is your English better now? How? (Is your grammar better? Do you know more words? Do you understand better?)

Start like this:

Dear _____ ,

I'm writing to you from [name of place]. I'm taking an English class here. The class is ...

11 Speak

a Read these questions and make notes of your answers.

- What goals do you have for learning English?
  I want to learn 20 new words per week.
  I want to find three interesting texts on the Internet per week.
- Why do you want to improve your English?
  I want to be able to understand the words of my favorite songs better.
  I want to be able to watch movies in English.
- How difficult/easy is it for you to speak English in class?
- What else can you do to learn English better?
  I can try to speak more English in class.
  I can read more in English.

b Discuss your answers in small groups. Then report to the class.

For your portfolio

10 We're going on vacation.

* Present continuous for future arrangements
* Vocabulary: future time expressions, vacation activities

1 Read and listen

a Look at this magazine article with ideas for adventure vacations for families. Which of these vacations looks the most interesting? Say why.

b ▶ CD2 T08 Listen to the radio show *Vacation Dreams*. Which of the places do the people go to? Write the numbers in the boxes.

Debbie ☐　　Mark ☐
Monica ☐

Family vacations can be fun!

Tour operators are now organizing real adventure vacations for families with teens.

1 Camping in the desert

Rocks, sand and wildlife – so many things that you can see in the desert in Turkey!

2 Diving in the Atlantic Ocean

Near the islands in the Florida Keys, you can swim with some of the most beautiful aquatic life in the world.

3 Kayaking in Ontario

Join us in Ontario, Canada, as we kayak down the Grand River.

4 Volunteering

There's a lot of volunteer work to choose from. How about helping the sea turtles in Costa Rica?

5 Seeing the delights of a winter wonderland

The cold weather doesn't bother you? Then come and have fun with a dog team pulling you across the snow in Alaska!

c ▶ CD2 T09 Listen to Sara talking to her friend Anna about her vacation plans. Complete the dialogue with the correct present continuous forms.

Sara: Hey, Anna! How's your day going?

Anna: Good! My mom and I are planning the family vacation.

Sara: Excellent! Where are you going?

Anna: Well, listen to this! We're ¹ _____ to Costa Rica!

Sara: Wow! Really? When?

Anna: In two months. We're ² _____ on May 3.

Sara: How are you getting there?

Anna: First we're ³ _____ to San José.

Sara: Oh. And are you ⁴ _____ in San José?

Anna: Oh, no! We're ⁵ _____ from there to Talamanca. And ... this is the best part! We're ⁶ _____ some work at a sea turtle conservation center!

Sara: Amazing! What are you ⁷ _____ there?

Anna: We're ⁸ _____ the sea turtles. We're ⁹ _____ things like cleaning the beach and taking care of baby turtles.

Sara: It sounds great! Is all your family ¹⁰ _____ with you?

Anna: Yes! But it's a little expensive. My dad almost fainted when he heard how much we're paying.

② Grammar

✷ Present continuous for future arrangements

a Underline other examples of the present continuous in the dialogue in Exercise 1c.

We're going to Costa Rica.
We're leaving on May 3.

> **RULE:** We often use the present continuous to talk about plans and arrangements for the future.

b Complete the sentences.

Use the present continuous form of the verbs.

1 I *'m visiting* (visit) my grandparents in Rome next year.

2 Come to our place next Saturday. We _____ (have) a party.

3 Mom _____ (take) my sister to New York on Thursday. They _____ (leave) early in the morning.

4 A: _____ you _____ (go) out tonight?
  B: No, I _____ (stay) at home.

5 My brother _____ (not go) on vacation with us this year. He _____ (work) in a store for six weeks.

6 I have toothache, so I _____ (see) the dentist tomorrow.

③ Vocabulary

✷ Future time expressions

a Here are some expressions we can use to talk about the future. How do you say them in your language?

> tomorrow
> next week/Saturday/ month/weekend
> in two/five days
> the day after tomorrow
> the week after next
> on Saturday morning / Sunday afternoon

b Answer the questions.

1 What day is the day after tomorrow?

2 What day is it in three days?

3 How many days is it until next Sunday?

4 What month is the month after next?

④ Speak

a Tell a partner what you're doing:

● this evening

● on Sunday morning

● next summer

b Now work with another partner. Tell him/her what you and your friend are doing.

A: *This evening I'm staying at home to watch my new DVD.*

B: *My friend is going to the Internet café on Sunday morning.*

5 Read

a What do you know about South Africa? Read the questions and (circle) your answers. If you don't know the answers, guess.

1 What is the capital of South Africa?
   a Cape Town   b Pretoria   c Johannesburg

2 What's the population of Cape Town?
   a about 3,500,000   b about 2,000,000
   c about 10,000,000

3 How many tourists visit Cape Town every year?
   a about 1,000,000   b about 5,000,000
   c about 2,000,000

4 What might you see at Boulders Beach?
   a shipwrecks   b penguins   c sharks

b Now read the text and check your answers to the questions in Exercise 5a.

c Find an adjective in the text to describe these things.

the beaches: _____
the shopping: _____
the settings: _____
the climate: _____

Welcome to Cape Town – the city that has everything!

About two million tourists visit Cape Town every year. It isn't the capital city (that's Pretoria), and it isn't the biggest city either (that's Johannesburg), but Cape Town is South Africa's most popular city with tourists for its many attractions, sights and activities. From the beautiful scenery and sunny beaches to great shopping in the downtown area, Cape Town has something for everyone. In fact, a vacation in Cape Town is unforgettable!

Adventure & outdoors

For the adventure, outdoor or sports fan, Cape Town has a range of activities from hiking, climbing and parachuting to diving and golf – all combined with fantastic settings and sunny skies.

Water sports & diving

Cape Town's beaches are ideal for water sports, including surfing, windsurfing and kayaking. Scuba diving is also popular. The many shipwrecks along the coastline offer some excellent dives. The more adventurous diver can even try shark cage diving to get eye-to-eye with a great white!

If you aren't so adventurous, try a visit to Boulders Beach. It's part of a conservation area for the African penguin. You can walk around on wooden paths and watch the penguins in their natural habitat. It's great for swimming and exploring, too, if you don't mind coming face-to-face with a penguin or two!

A few facts & figures

Cape Town's climate is pleasant. In summer, it's about 26 °C (and remember, mid-summer here is January!), and the winter temperatures don't usually fall below 10 °C. The local currency is the rand. There are one hundred cents to every rand. The three main languages are Xhosa, English and Afrikaans. The population of Cape Town is about 3.5 million.

6 Vocabulary

⭐ Vacation activities

a ▶ **CD2 T10** Write the names of the activities under the pictures. Then listen, check and repeat.

hiking   rock climbing   parachuting   scuba diving   golfing   surfing   windsurfing   kayaking
canoeing   snorkeling   ~~sailing~~   camping   sightseeing   sunbathing   horseback riding

sailing

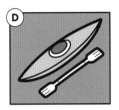

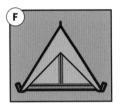

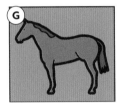

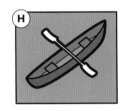

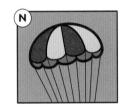

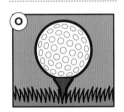

b Work with a partner. Which of the activities do you like doing on vacation?

A: *I like windsurfing, but I'm not very good at it.*

B: *I don't like sunbathing. It's boring.*

c Fill in each space with a verb from the box.

rent   travel   stay   ~~buy~~   spend

1   __buy__ souvenirs / presents / postcards / stamps

2   _____ in a hotel / in a bed and breakfast / at a campsite / in a youth hostel / at home

3   _____ to Ireland / by ferry / by car / by plane / by train / by bus

4   _____ your vacation (in South Africa) / some time (on the beach) / two weeks (in Greece)

5   _____ a car / a boat / a bike / a surfboard

7 Speak

a Make a list of all the different kinds of vacations and vacation places in this unit.

b Imagine your family is planning a vacation. Look at your list and choose a place to visit.

c Make notes about your vacation plans:

- Where are you going?
- How long and where are you staying?
- What are you planning to do there?
- How are you getting there?

d Work with a partner. Ask and answer questions.

A: *Where are you going for your next vacation?*

B: *We're going to ...*

8 Pronunciation

▶ **CD2 T11 and T12** Pronunciation section starts on page 114.

Having fun?

9 ▶ CD2 T13 **Read and listen**

a Look at the photostory. Where are they? How do they feel in the first photograph? How do they feel in the last photograph? Who does Kim talk to? Read and listen to find the answers.

①

Alex: This isn't fun at all.

Emily: I'm not enjoying myself.

Matt: You're not the only one.

Kim: Wait a sec. I have a call.

Kim: Oh, hi, Dad! ... Yeah, fine thanks. What? No, we're all having a really good time! No, don't worry. It's a little cold, but we're having a lot of fun. OK. Bye!

②

Alex: Are you crazy, Kim?

Matt: Us? Having fun? In this cold weather?

Emily: I can't believe you said that!

④

Kim: Look, there's no way I'm telling my dad that we're having a bad time. And I'm not going to tell people at school, either. And anyway, if we aren't having fun, it's our fault, isn't it?

③

⑤

Matt: Let's play a game, then.

Emily: Or sing a song.

Alex: Or we could make ice cream!

Kim: Very funny! But, see? Now we really *are* having a good time!

b Match the beginnings and endings to make a summary of the story.

1 Alex, Emily, Matt and Kim
2 Kim's dad
3 Kim tells her dad that they
4 Alex, Matt and Emily
5 Kim doesn't want people
6 In the end, they all start

a calls Kim.
b to know that they aren't having a good time.
c having a good time.
d aren't enjoying themselves.
e are having a good time.
f are very surprised by what Kim says.

10 Everyday English

a Find expressions 1–6 in the photostory. Who says them? How do you say the underlined parts in your language?

1 This isn't fun <u>at all</u>.

2 <u>Wait a sec</u>.

3 No, <u>don't worry</u>.

4 I'm not going to tell people at school, <u>either</u>.

5 <u>it's</u> our <u>fault</u>

6 Let's play a game, <u>then</u>.

b Read the dialogue. Use the <u>underlined</u> parts of the expressions in Exercise 10a to complete it.

Sam: Let's go shopping. There's a great new music store in town.

Louise: I can't. I don't have any money ¹ _at all_ .

Sam: Well, ask your parents for some money, ² _____ .

Louise: I can't. They gave me some money yesterday. I spent it all last night, though.

Sam: OK. So ³ _____ your _____ that you don't have any money.

Louise: Absolutely. ⁴ _____ . Maybe I can ask my grandparents.

Sam: Good idea.

Louise: No. I can't ask them, ⁵ _____ . They're in Brazil on vacation.

Sam: OK. ⁶ _____ . I'll go shopping alone. No problem!

Discussion box

1 Kim says, "If we aren't having fun, it's our fault, isn't it?" What is your opinion about this?

2 How does the weather influence *your* feelings? Give examples.

3 Think of a situation that wasn't that great but you still had fun. Say what happened.

---

11 Improvisation

Work with a partner. Take two minutes to prepare a short role play. Try to use some of the expressions from Exercise 10a. Do not write the text, just agree on your ideas for a short scene. Then act it out.

Roles: Matt and Alex

Situation: At Matt's place, a week later

Basic idea: Matt and Alex want to play soccer, but it's very cold outside.

Use one of these sentences to start the conversation:

Matt: I can't believe it. We want to play soccer, but it's so cold outside.

Alex: I think we should play soccer even if it's cold.

12 Reach Out

a Imagine you are going on a camping trip. Look at these things and put them in order of importance from 1–10. (1 = very important / 10 = not important). Then discuss in small groups. Explain your reasons for each object.

b Watch Episode 5 and find out about Emily, Kim, Alex and Matt's camping trip.

13 Write

a Imagine you got this email from your friend Cynthia. How does she feel? Why?

Hi, (your name)!

I'm so excited. Guess what? It's my dad's 40th birthday next month, so he's taking us all to London for a vacation! Cool, right?

We're flying over on Thursday evening. As soon as we arrive, we're going on a tour of the city. They say London is really beautiful at night, and I'm really looking forward to seeing all those famous places.

On Friday, we're going to the Tate Modern (the art gallery near the river Thames), and then to the Design Museum. It's not far from our hotel, so we're planning to walk there. In the afternoon, we're going on the London Eye. I can't wait to see the Houses of Parliament from up there!

Saturday is for shopping. There's no doubt about that! We're going to Portobello Road first. Then in the afternoon, we're visiting Harrod's – the most famous store in London! Dad's not very happy about it, but I'm sure he'll enjoy it once we're there.

On Sunday morning, we're going to Hyde Park, and we're flying home in the afternoon. It's my dream trip, and it's really happening!

Hope everything's OK with you.

Love, Cynthia

b Write back to Cynthia. In your email, tell her about a trip you are going on. Include this information about the arrangement:

- where and when you are going
- who you are going with
- how you are traveling
- where you are staying
- what you are doing there
- how long you are staying

14 Last but not least: more speaking

Work with a partner.

Student A: Look at the card below.

Student B: Turn to page 117.

Ask questions to find out when and where your partner is going on vacation and what they are going to do there.

Student A

Destination: Australia

Dates: November 8 – December 6

Travel arrangements: Fly to Sydney (Kingsford Smith) International Airport

Hotel: Hilton Sydney

Trips: Sydney Harbor Cruise, Blue Mountain Tour

Activities: Surfing off Bondi Beach

Check your progress

1 Grammar

a Complete the sentences. Use the comparative or superlative form of the adjectives.

1 Today is _the longest_ (long) day of the year.

2 For me, geography is _____ (difficult) than math. It's difficult for me to remember facts about countries.

3 History is _____ (easy) subject at school.

4 I feel awful! This is _____ (bad) day of my life!

5 I don't argue with Jo, because he's _____ (big) than me.

6 Sally is _____ (good) than me at art.

7 I think my grades will be _____ (bad) this year than last year.

8 If you want to be fit, a healthy diet and a lot of exercise are _____ (important) things. ☐ 7

b Look at Linda's diary. Write sentences about the things she's doing next weekend.

> **Saturday**
> 10:00 driving lesson
> 3:00 meet Gerard at café
> 6:00 movie with Sue
> **Sunday**
> 12:30 lunch with Wendy
> 5:00 homework
> 7:30 cousins arrive from Canada!

Saturday

1 At 10:00, she _'s taking a driving lesson._

2 At 3:00, she _____ .

3 At 6:00, she and Sue _____ .

Sunday

4 At 12:30, she and Wendy _____ .

5 At 5:00, _____ .

6 At 7:30, _____ . ☐ 5

2 Vocabulary

a Complete the sentences with the words in the box.

> imitate   translate   ~~make mistakes~~
> look up   accent   mean   guess
> communicate

1 When I speak English, I sometimes _make mistakes_ in grammar, but I can still _____ with English speakers.

2 Excuse me, what does this word _____ ?

3 I want my pronunciation to be better, so I listen to CDs and _____ the speakers.

4 For homework, our teacher sometimes gives us texts in English and we have to _____ them into our language.

5 My father speaks English well, but he has a very strong _____ .

6 When I don't know a word, I try to _____ the meaning. If I can't do that, I _____ the word in my dictionary. ☐ 7

b Write the vacation activities in the lists.

> rock climbing   windsurfing   ~~swimming~~
> camping   horseback riding   sightseeing
> snorkeling   canoeing   surfing
> sunbathing

in/on water	not in/on water
swimming	

☐ 9

How did you do?

Check your score.

Total score	😊 Very good	😐 OK	😟 Not very good
☐ 28			
Grammar	12 – 10	9 – 8	7 or less
Vocabulary	16 – 13	12 –10	9 or less

* *will/won't*
* Vocabulary: expressions to talk about the future, expressions to talk about future technology

Getting the future wrong!

People love reading predictions. They love looking into the future. They want to know what will or won't happen tomorrow, next week, next year and in the next century!

But predictions are not always right. They can go very, very wrong! Here are some of our favorite predictions that went wrong.

* In 1859, a man named Edwin Drake wanted to drill for oil. A worker said, "Drill for oil? You mean drill into the ground to find oil? You're crazy."

* In 1872, the U.S. president Rutherford B. Hayes looked at Alexander Bell's new telephone and said, "An amazing invention, but who would ever want to use one?"

* In 1899, a top British scientist said, "Radio has no future."

1 Read and listen

a ▶ **CD2 T14** Look at the predictions for the future. Match the predictions with the people in the pictures. Then listen and check your answers.

1 "I think they'll have special machines that do X-rays of cars so that when they break down, we can find out immediately what's wrong with them."

2 "I believe that one day we'll be able to totally control the weather. We won't have bad storms and hurricanes anymore."

3 "One day, there won't be any real toys anymore. Kids will play with virtual toys. I think that'll be very sad."

4 "I'm sure one day scientists will invent little robots that are so cheap we can all afford to buy one and keep it at home to help in the house and stuff."

5 "In the future, there will be some great inventions. I bet very rich people will have their own personal space rockets, so they can fly off into space whenever they feel like it!"

b Read the predictions again. Mark them: (1) I totally believe this will happen (2) I'm not sure this will happen (3) This won't happen. Now compare your views with other students.

c Now read the text. Did you know about any of these predictions that went wrong? Which is your favorite prediction?

d ▶ **CD2 T15** Read the text again and listen. Complete the sentences to express what people said.

1 A movie producer said that television ...

2 The boss of a record company said that the Beatles ...

3 The boss of a big computer company said that no one would want ...

4 A U.S. president said that not many people would ...

e Discuss in class.

Write three predictions for the future – two you believe will happen and one crazy one. Don't tell your partner which one you don't believe will happen. Read them to each other and try to guess which one is the "crazy" one.

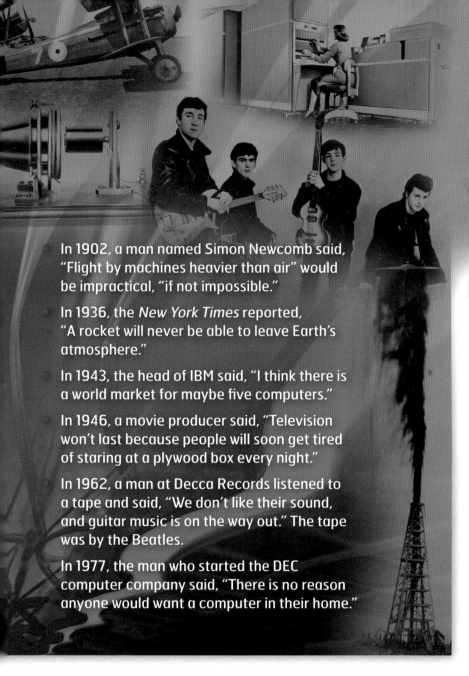

In 1902, a man named Simon Newcomb said, "Flight by machines heavier than air" would be impractical, "if not impossible."

In 1936, the *New York Times* reported, "A rocket will never be able to leave Earth's atmosphere."

In 1943, the head of IBM said, "I think there is a world market for maybe five computers."

In 1946, a movie producer said, "Television won't last because people will soon get tired of staring at a plywood box every night."

In 1962, a man at Decca Records listened to a tape and said, "We don't like their sound, and guitar music is on the way out." The tape was by the Beatles.

In 1977, the man who started the DEC computer company said, "There is no reason anyone would want a computer in their home."

2 Grammar

✱ will/won't

a Look at the examples. <u>Underline</u> examples of *will/'ll* and *won't* in the texts in Exercise 1.

I think they'll have special machines.
Five people will buy a computer.   It won't work.

b Complete the table and the rule.

Affirmative	Negative	Question	Short answers
I/you/we/they/he/she/it _____ (will) come	I/you/we/they/he/she/it _____ (will not) come	_____ I/you/we/they/he/she/it come?	Yes, I/you/we/they/he/she/it _____ . No, I/you/we/they/he/_____ she/it (will not).

RULE: We use _____ (*will*) or _____ (*will not*) + base form to make predictions about the future.

c Complete the dialogue with *'ll*, *will* or *won't* and a verb from the box.

> stay   go   see   give
> be   ~~get~~   help

Tori: Oh, Pete, it's the math test tomorrow!
I hate math. I'm sure I
¹ *won't get* the answers right!

Pete: Don't worry, you
² _____ fine! You got a good grade on your last test.

Tori: Yes, but this is more difficult. I really don't feel well. Maybe I ³ _____ to school tomorrow. I ⁴ _____ in bed all day.

Pete: That ⁵ _____ you. The teacher ⁶ _____ you the test on Wednesday.

Tori: You're right. But what can I do?

Pete: Look, why don't I come over to your place this afternoon after school? We can study for the math test together. You ⁷ _____ it's not so difficult.

Tori: Oh, thanks, Pete.

d Work with a partner. Act out the dialogue in Exercise 2c.

3 Pronunciation

▶ **CD2 T16** Pronunciation sections starts on page 114.

4 Listen

▶ CD2 T17 Listen to Sally and Patrick talking about the future, and complete the first two columns of the table. Check (✓) the things they think will happen and write an "X" for the things they think won't happen.

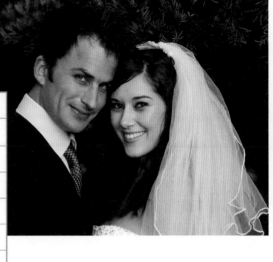

	Sally	Patrick	Me	My partner
get married	✓			
have children				
go to college				
get a good job				
learn to drive				
become famous				

5 Vocabulary

✱ Expressions to talk about the future

a Sally says, "I hope to get a good job." Does she want to get a good job? Is she sure she'll get one? How do you say "I hope to" in your language?

b Look at these sentences from the dialogue. Write the underlined phrases in the correct column.

1   I think I'll get married.
2   I'll probably go to college.
3   I don't think I'll live abroad.
4   I doubt I'll be famous.

5   Maybe I'll get married.
6   I'm sure I won't have children.
7   I hope to get a good job.
8   I'm sure I'll learn to drive.

A I believe this will happen	B I believe this won't happen	C I think it's possible that this will happen
I think I'll ...		

6 Speak

a Look at the table in Exercise 4. Complete the *Me* column with your own answers.

b Work with a partner. Guess what your partner's answer will be to the questions. Then ask him/her the questions and complete the *My Partner* column of the table.

A: *Will you get married and have children?*   B: *Yes, I'll probably get married, and I hope to have children.*

c Compare your answers with other students.

7 Listen: a song

a ▶ **CD2 T18** Listen to the song and answer the questions.

When I'm Sixty-four
The Beatles

If I'd been out till quarter to three,
Would you lock the door?
Will you still need me, will you still feed me,
When I'm sixty-four?

You'll be older too,
And if you say the word,
I could stay with you.

I could be handy, mending a fuse
When your lights have gone.
You can knit a sweater by the fireside,
Sunday morning go for a ride.

Doing the garden, digging the weeds,
Who could ask for more?
Will you still need me, will you still feed me,
When I'm sixty-four?

Every summer we can rent a cottage
In the Isle of Wight, if it's not too dear.
We shall scrimp and save.
Grandchildren on your knee,
Vera, Chuck and Dave.

Send me a postcard, drop me a line,
Stating point of view.
Indicate precisely what you mean to say,
Yours sincerely, wasting away

Give me your answer, fill in a form,
Mine for evermore.
Will you still need me, will you still feed me
When I'm sixty-four?

b Match the words with their definitions.

1 lock | *i* |
2 feed | |
3 handy | |
4 mend a fuse | |
5 dig the weeds | |
6 cottage | |
7 scrimp and save | |
8 drop me a line | |
9 waste away | |
10 fill in a form | |

a   try hard to save money
b   repair something electrical
c   take out plants you don't want
    in the garden
d   a small house in the country
e   give food to
f   write to me
g   useful, practical
h   write down official information
i   close with a key
j   get very thin because you're sick
    or don't eat

c Listen to the song again and choose the best answer for the questions.

1   What is the singer trying to do in the song?
    a   get a gardening job
    b   tell his wife to spend less money
    c   ask someone to marry him
    d   ask for food

2   The singer:
    a   thinks his wife is angry with him.
    b   imagines their future life together.
    c   has three grandchildren.
    d   wants to know if his girlfriend can
        cook and knit.

3   The singer imagines that their future
    will be:
    a   simple and modest.
    b   busy.
    c   hard work.
    d   one long vacation.

d ▶ **CD2 T18** Play the song again and sing along.

Culture in mind

8 Read and listen

a Work in small groups.

How are computers and phones different from how they were 50 years ago? What will they be like in the future? Use the pictures on the page to help you.

b ▶ **CD2 T19** Listen and answer the questions.

1 Which technology helps the environment?
2 Which two items go in your body?
3 What might be different about plastic arms and legs in the future?
4 Where will people go to school in the future?

The Future of Technology

Fifty years ago, people didn't imagine a computer in most homes or a telephone smaller than a hand. What new technology will be here in the next 50 years? Many people have predictions about future technology. Here are just a few.

Communication

Imagine a phone that can read your mind. Some scientists predict cell phones will become our "virtual assistants" in the future. They think phones will let people know who they want to talk to, they'll control the temperature in homes and they'll automatically download music people like.

Today, people can have conversations on the Internet using video. In the future, scientists predict we'll have 3-D conversations. You'll be able to stay in your home and talk to a virtual image of your friend.

Some scientists think we'll have Internet implants or computer chips in our bodies that allow us to use the Internet without traditional laptop or desktop computers.

Health

Scientists are sure there will be ways to cure more diseases in the future. Some scientists hope to predict what diseases people might get, and cure those diseases before people get them.

Today, some people have plastic body parts such as arms and legs. In the future, people may actually be able to feel with these parts. Some doctors predict that there will also be more artificial parts inside the body, like plastic muscles.

Education

Imagine not going to school! Some people think that in the future everyone will learn from home. Students will take all of their classes online. Others think students will be able to download information for school on their Internet implants!

Transportation

Computers in the future might tell people which roads to take to get somewhere. They will do this before traffic gets bad on certain roads. Imagine a world with no traffic jams!

Cars in the future will probably be better for the environment. Scientists doubt cars will use air for fuel, but they think there will be many electric cars in the future.

Some people think these changes will be good, and others think they won't be. Either way, new technology will affect our way of life in the future.

9 Vocabulary

✱ Expressions to talk about future technology

a (Circle) the correct meaning for each of these words from the text.

1 to imagine (verb)
   a to think about something that happened
   (b) to think about something that could happen

2 to read your mind (verb phrase)
   a to know what you're thinking
   b to turn something on

3 automatically
   a done by a machine
   b done by a person

4 virtual (adjective)
   a not real
   b friendly

5 to predict (verb)
   a to ask someone what will happen
   b to say what you think will happen

6 to cure (verb)
   a to make healthy
   b to hurt

7 implant (noun)
   a something put in the body
   b a type of phone

8 artificial (adjective)
   a outside the body
   b made by people

b Use words in Exercise 9a to complete these sentences. You may need to change the form of the words.

1 What are you thinking? I can't _____ !

2 Scientists _____ there will be better heart _____ in the future.

3 My coffee maker turns off _____ .

4 _____ a world in which doctors _____ every disease!

5 This computer game has a great _____ city.

6 I have _____ plants in my house, so I don't have to water them.

10 Write

a Read this student's predictions about life in the future. Complete the text with words from the box.

> will be   be-like   won't be   will happen
> They'll do   will learn   we'll recycle   will find

What will life [1] ___*be like*___ one hundred years from now? I don't know, of course. But this is what I think [2] _____ .

First, I think that computers [3] _____ much more important in our lives. There [4] _____ any televisions or DVD players or things like that. I think all those things will be part of a computer. And everything in our house will be controled by computers. I believe scientists [5] _____ a way to make computers talk and think, just like people. That's scary!

Also there won't be any more pollution. Governments will find ways to stop pollution and [6] _____ everything.

Finally, I think that there won't be any schools. Some people say teachers will be robots in the future, but I don't think that's true. I think kids [7] _____ at home using their computers. [8] _____ everything online. (Great, because when they're bored, they can have a little fun and play a few online games!)

That's what I think about life in the future. I think it'll be very different, but very exciting!

b Now write your own text (150 words) with the title, What will life be like two hundred years from now?

11 Speak

a Work with a partner. Talk about how the technology in the text on page 76 will affect life in the future. Discuss these questions:

- What do you think of each prediction for technology in the future?
- Will the technology be good or bad for people?
- How will life change if each prediction comes true?

b Invent a new technology for the future. It can be as realistic or crazy as you like.

For your portfolio

UNIT 11   77

* *too* + adjective; adverbs
* Vocabulary: the weather

1 Read and listen

a Look at the pictures. What do they show?

b Read the text quickly to find out why the river was important to Juliane.

JUNGLE SURVIVAL

On December 24, 1971, 17-year-old Juliane Köpcke got on a plane with her mother in Lima, Peru, to fly to another city to meet her father.

Over the Amazon jungle, there was a thunderstorm. The rain fell heavily and there was a strong wind. And then lightning hit the plane at 3,000 meters, and it exploded. Juliane fell quickly through the air in her seat and hit the trees hard. For three hours, she was unconscious. When she woke up, her right arm was cut, her shoulder hurt badly and she couldn't see out of one eye. She was alone. But she was alive!

Pucallpa

PERU

Lima

Juliane's father was a biologist, and when she was young, he taught her how to survive in the jungle. She found a small river and walked slowly along it. "If I follow the river," she thought, "I'll find people." The river also gave her clean water to drink. It was extremely hot, but the river water kept her cool. Sometimes she had to swim in the river because it was too deep to walk in. There were crocodiles in the water, but they didn't attack her! There was fruit on some trees, but she didn't eat it because she knew it was too dangerous.

Juliane walked for 10 days. At night, she stopped to sleep because it was too dark to walk. Ten days after the crash, she found a small hut by the river. There were some woodcutters in the hut. They cleaned her cuts carefully, and the next day, they carried her down the river. A plane took her safely back to the city of Pucallpa.

Juliane was the only person who survived the plane crash. The other 91 people, including her mother, all died.

The movie director, Werner Herzog, had a ticket to travel on the plane, but missed it. Thirty years later, he made a documentary movie called *Wings of Hope* about Juliane and her incredible story.

c The title of the text is "Jungle Survival." Work with a partner and talk about the difficulties of surviving in the jungle.

Juliane Köpcke in April 1972

d ▶ **CD2 T13** Now read the text again and listen. Complete the sentences with words from the text.

1 Rain can fall h_____ .
2 Juliane fell through the air q_____ .
3 She walked s_____ along the river.
4 If you arrive somewhere without any problems, you arrive s_____ .

e Discuss in class.

1 Would you like to see the movie *Wings of Hope*? Why / why not?
2 Why do you think Werner Herzog decided to make a movie about the plane crash?

2 Grammar

✱ *too* + adjective

a Match the two parts of the sentences. How do you say the underlined words in your language?

1 There was fruit on some trees, but she didn't eat it because
2 At night she stopped to sleep because
3 She swam in the river because

a the water was <u>too deep</u> to walk in.
b she knew it was <u>too dangerous</u>.
c it was <u>too dark</u> to walk.

b Complete the sentences with *too* and an adjective.

1 I can't watch the rest of the movie. I'm *too tired* ! So I'm going to bed.
2 It's _____ to go swimming today. We'll freeze!
3 Grandma doesn't want to come to the party. She says she's _____ for parties and dancing!
4 I want an MP3 player, but they're _____ . I don't have that much money.
5 I didn't like the movie. It was _____ . I only like short movies.
6 He didn't answer any of the questions. They were all _____ .

c Complete the sentences. Use *too* or *very* and a word from the box.

old   big   heavy

1 Look at that house. It's _____ .

2 I think this hat is _____ .

3 I can't lift it. It's _____ .

4 These bags are _____ .

5 These paintings are _____ .

6 We can't use this phone now. It's _____ .

3 Vocabulary

✳ The weather

a Complete the sentences with the words in the box.

> sun thunder lightning
> hot shower ~~wind~~

1 It was a very cold day, and the ___wind___ was really cold, too.

2 _____ hit that tree six months ago.

3 Don't sit out in the _____ for too long; you'll burn.

4 Gosh! What was that noise? I think it was _____ .

5 It's much too _____ to go for a walk right now.

6 It didn't rain heavily. It was just a _____ .

b ▶ CD2 T21 Listen and complete the weather forecast.

And now for today's forecast. In the Baltimore area, the weather will be ¹ ___warm___ with temperatures of around 18 °C. Although the sun will shine for a while, we can expect some strong ² _____ this afternoon. And that will make it feel pretty cool.

Further north in the New York City area, things won't be too good. After last night's ³ _____ , New York is going to be very ⁴ _____ with an expected high of about 14 °C. But no more ⁵ _____ and ⁶ _____ today, at least. And finally, in Boston, it will be ⁷ _____ for part of the morning and then ⁸ _____ later on. But not snowing like it was yesterday. The roads should be safer once the fog clears.

c Write three sentences to describe what the weather will be like tomorrow where you are. Compare your predictions with a partner and check tomorrow.

4 Grammar

✳ Adverbs

a Look at the examples from the text on page 78 and complete the rule.

*The rain fell **heavily**.*
*It was **extremely** hot.*
*A plane took her **safely** back to the city of Pucallpa.*

> **RULE:** Adverbs describe adjectives and _____ .
> To form a regular adverb, we usually add _____ to the adjective. If the adjective ends with *y*, change the *y* to _____ before adding _____ .

b Underline more examples of adverbs in the text on page 78.

c Complete the tables.

Adjectives	Regular adverbs
slow	_slowly_
bad	_____
loud	_____
quiet	_____
lucky	_____
easy	_____

Adjectives	Irregular adverbs
fast	_fast_
good	_____
early	_early_
late	_late_
hard	_____

d Complete the sentences. Use adverbs from the tables in Exercise 4c.

1 I play the piano ___badly___ , but I can sing pretty _____ .
2 She talks very _____ . It's often difficult to hear her.
3 They missed the train because they arrived _____ .
4 If you want to pass your exam, you need to study _____ .

5 Speak

a Work with a partner. Ask and answer the questions.

1 Do you study better early or late in the day?
2 Do you prefer to walk quickly or slowly?
3 Do you play your music loudly or quietly?
4 Do you do your homework slowly or quickly?

b Tell your partner about other things you do. Use the adverbs in the box.

> fast   slowly   well   badly   loudly   carefully   lazily   impatiently

A: *I can speak French very well.*

B: *I play tennis well, but I play golf badly.*

6 Pronunciation

> ► CD2 T22 and T23   Pronunciation section starts on page 114.

7 Listen and speak

a Look at the pictures of Hermann Maier. Work with a partner and put the pictures in order. Then tell the story of Hermann Maier's life together.

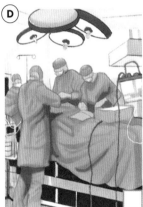

b ► CD2 T24   Listen to a boy and his father talking about Hermann Maier. Check your version of the story.

c ► CD2 T24   Listen again and match the two parts of the sentences.

1	When Hermann was 15,	a	Hermann got on the Austrian skiing team.
2	For a time,	b	a car hit him.
3	In 1996,	c	he was sent home from skiing school.
4	In 1998,	d	he won the World Cup!
5	In 2001,	e	Hermann worked as a bricklayer.
6	In 2004,	f	Hermann won an Olympic Gold medal.

d Work with a partner. Take turns being Hermann Maier. Tell each other your life story. Use your own words and try to describe your (Hermann's) feelings.

Keep running.

8 ▶ **CD2 T25** **Read and listen**

a Look at the photostory. What are Emily and Alex doing? Why isn't Emily very happy? What does Alex tell her to do? Read and listen to find the answers.

1

Alex: This is OK. In fact, it's really fun!

Emily: Yeah. It's not bad.

Alex: Hey, are you OK, Emily?

2

Emily: Well, no, not really. I have this pain right here. Near my stomach.

Alex: Oh, no.

Emily: Yeah, it really hurts. I'm going to stop.

3

Alex: No. You have to keep running. Press with your hand, right where it hurts. But whatever you do, don't stop!

4

Emily: Keep running? Are you sure?

Alex: Yeah, I know it sounds weird, in a way, but it's the best thing to do.

5

Emily: Well, Alex, you were right. The pain's gone!

Alex: See? You just keep going! But ... maybe we could stop in a minute? I'm kind of tired now!

Emily: Oh, Alex, don't be such a wimp!

b There is something wrong in each sentence. Put a line through the incorrect information and change it.

1 Alex thinks running is ~~horrible~~. *really fun*

2 Emily has a pain near her neck. _____

3 Emily is going to cry. _____

4 Alex says that Emily has to stop running. _____

5 Alex says that not stopping is the wrong thing to do. _____

6 Emily's pain doesn't go away. _____

7 Alex wants to stop running now. _____

9 Everyday English

a Find expressions 1–6 in the photostory. Who says them? How do you say them in your language?

1 In fact, …
2 … not really.
3 Are you sure?
4 … in a way …
5 … the best thing to do.
6 … in a minute.

b Read the dialogues. Use the expressions in Exercise 9a to complete them.

1 A: David? Can you come and help me?

   B: _In a minute_ . I'm working.

2 A: I have a terrible headache.

   B: Well, take an aspirin and go to bed. That's
   _____ .

3 A: This CD is by Jordin Sparks.

   B: _____ ? I think it's Taylor Swift.

4 A: Would you like to watch a DVD with me?

   B: No, _____ , thanks. I have to do my homework.

5 A: This is a great movie.

   B: You're right.
   _____ , it's the best movie I've ever seen!

6 A: Jake didn't come to the party.

   B: I know, and _____ I'm glad. He's a really bad boy sometimes!

> **Discussion box**
> 1 What do you think about running as a sport?
> 2 When did you last have a pain while playing a sport? What happened?

10 Improvisation

Work with a partner. Take two minutes to prepare a short role play. Try to use some of the expressions from Exercise 9a. Do not write the text, just agree on your ideas for a short scene. Then act it out.

Roles: Emily and Alex

Situation: A minute later

Basic idea: Alex has fallen down. Emily is worried.

Use one of these sentences to start the conversation:

Emily: Are you OK?   **Alex:** I can't believe it!

11 Reach Out DVD Episode 6

a Complete the sentences with the words from the box. Use a dictionary if necessary. Then say what you think Episode 6 is about.

b Watch the DVD and see if you were right.

> take   celebrate   bet   training
> into   down   ~~raise~~

1 We're running to _raise_ money for the senior center.
2 I'm not really _____ sports.
3 I _____ they're great runners.
4 Don't worry. I can _____ care of myself.
5 You stopped _____ with me.
6 I don't let people _____ .
7 Come on! Let's _____ !

12 Write

a Imagine you got this email from your friend, Spiro, who is studying English in a language school. Why is he unhappy?

Hi, (your name)!

How are you? I'm not feeling great right now. I'm finding English very difficult. I hate it, and I really want to give it up. My parents say it's important and I have to keep going. I can't speak English very well, and I get terrible grades on my tests. Do you have any ideas? Help me, please!

Spiro

b Complete the email reply to Spiro. Give him some ideas about learning English. Use some of these phrases.

I think it's a good idea to ...

Try to ...   Remember to ...

Why don't you ...?

... is good/useful/helpful, because ...

... will help you to ...

Hi, Spiro!

I'm sorry you're feeling bad, but please don't worry about English, and don't give up! I have some ideas to help you.

....

13 Last but not least: more speaking

Work with a partner.

Student A: Look at the card below.

Student B: Turn to page 117.

Ask questions and answer your partner's to complete the information.

Famous athlete

Full name: ....

Date of birth: ....

Place of birth: ....

Sport: ....

Began playing when ....

.... ,

In 1995, he started ....

.... ,

In 1999, he ....

.... ,

In 2008, he ....

....

Famous athlete

Full name: Marta Viera da Silva
Date of birth: February 19, 1986
Place of birth: Dois Riachos, Brazil
Sport: women's soccer

Started to play for a Brazilian team, Vasco da Gama, at the age of 14.

Scored 6 goals for her country in 2004 Women's World Championship.

Also in 2004, started to play for a Swedish team, Umeà.

In 2006 and 2007, she became Player of the Year.

Check your progress

1 Grammar

a Complete the sentences with *will* or *won't*.

1 My train is running late, so I __won't__ be home before seven o'clock.

2 Julie isn't feeling well. I don't think she _____ go to school today.

3 He's a really good actor. I'm sure he _____ become famous one day.

4 We can go to the beach tomorrow. I'm sure it _____ rain.

5 What do you think? _____ you go to college?

6 Kurt is in Tokyo, so he _____ be at the party tonight.

7 It's really hot today. I think I _____ go swimming this afternoon.

8 Tom's always so nice. He _____ get angry when he finds out.

9 A: _____ you come to the game tomorrow?

   B: Sorry, but I don't think I _____ have time. I _____ come to the one next week.

10 A: Pat _____ be happy when she sees that you have broken her computer.

   B: I know. I _____ tell her what happened as soon as she comes home.

   [12]

b Circle the correct words.

1 My parents are (angry) / angrily because I didn't do the dishes.

2 Our team lost yesterday. Everyone played *bad / badly.*

3 Last week's test was *easy / easily.*

4 My sister sings *good / well.*

5 Hurry up, Jill! Why are you walking so *slow / slowly*?

6 Last night I heard a *loud / loudly* noise outside my room.

7 It was a *slow / slowly* journey, and we arrived very *late / lately.*

8 The players were all too *slow / slowly.* That's why we lost the game.

9 His mom works so *hard / hardly.* She's *hard / hardly* at home.

   [10]

2 Vocabulary

a Circle the correct words.

1 I'll (probably) / sure get a good job.

2 Jin *doubts / hopes* to become a famous singer.

3 *Maybe / Don't think* she'll have children.

4 Nick *thinks / probably* they'll get married soon.

5 I'm *doubt / sure* he'll learn to drive.

6 We'll *doubt / probably* watch TV tonight.

7 I *doubt / sure* he'll come with us.

    [6]

b Use the words to complete the sentences.

> lightning   foggy   shower   thunder
> ~~wind~~   hot   rain   sun

1 There was such a strong __wind__ that some trees fell down.

2 The house on that hill burned down because it was struck by _____ .

3 There was heavy _____ for three days. The streets looked like rivers.

4 It didn't really rain very hard. It was only a _____ .

5 We didn't sit on the beach after 11:00 a.m. There was too much _____ , and it was too _____ .

6 I just heard some _____ from far away. I think there'll be a storm soon.

7 I couldn't see anything from my window this morning. It was really _____ outside!

   [7]

How did you do?

Check your score.

Total score	☺	☺	☹
[35]	Very good	OK	Not very good
Grammar	22 – 18	17 – 15	14 or less
Vocabulary	13 – 11	10 – 8	7 or less

13 Promises, promises

* *be going to* (intentions and predictions); *must/can't*
* Vocabulary: multi-word verbs (2), prepositions

1 Read and listen

a How do you celebrate the New Year in your country?

b Look at the text quickly. Find words or phrases with these meanings:

1 the day before January 1: *December 31* or ....

2 12 o'clock at night: ....

3 promises people make for the New Year: ....

c Read the text.

d ▶ CD2 T26 Now read the text again and listen. Answer the questions.

1 Where is Times Square?

2 What appears in Times Square just before midnight on December 31?

3 What do you hear at midnight in Times Square?

4 What happens to many New Year's resolutions?

2 Listen

▶ CD2 T27 Listen to Amy and her dad talking about their New Year's resolutions. Who says what? Write *A* (Amy), or *D* (Dad) next to each sentence.

1 I'm not going to eat unhealthy food anymore. ☐

2 I'm going to give up eating French fries. ☐

3 Mom and I are going to check out that new gym. ☐

4 I'm going to take up running. ☐

5 We're going to start up a business. ☐

6 I'm sure we can work something out. ☐

Celebrate New Year's Eve

It's almost midnight on December 31, in Times Square, in New York City. At 11:59, a sparkling crystal ball appears on the roof of 1 Times Square. The ball takes 60 seconds to drop. Then the clock strikes 12 and everyone cheers. About a million people in Times Square, millions around the U.S. and over a billion watching around the world, come together to say "good-bye" to the old year and "hello" to the new.

In the U.S., the new year is also a time for thinking about the changes you are going to make in your life. These are called "New Year's resolutions." People say, for example, that they are going to give up chocolate or take up a new sport. Of course, it's easy to make New Year's resolutions, but it's not so easy to keep them! Unfortunately, many New Year's resolutions have one thing in common. People break them before the new year is over!

3 Vocabulary

* Multi-word verbs (2)

▶ CD2 T28 Match the verbs with the definitions. Then listen, check and repeat.

1 take up   a go to a place to see what it is like

2 give up   b start doing something

3 look up   c cancel an event

4 call off   d stop doing something

5 work out   e find the answer to something

6 check out   f find out information about something from a book or computer

4 Grammar

✱ be going to: intentions

a Read the rule and complete the table.

RULE: We use *be going to* to talk about our intentions in the future (for example, *I'm going to eat more fruit.*). We use the present tense of **be** + *going to* + base form of the verb.

Affirmative	Negative	Questions	Short answers
I'm (am) going to change.	I'm not (am not) going to change.	Am I going to change?	Yes, I _____ . No, I'm **not**.
you/we/they 're (are) going to change	you/we/they _____ (are not) going to change	_____ you/we/they going to change?	Yes, you/we/they _____ . No, you/we/they **aren't**.
he/she/it's (is) going to change	he/she/it _____ (is not) going to change	_____ he/she/it going to change?	Yes, he/she/it **is**. No, he/she/it _____ .

b Complete the sentences about Amy and her dad. Use the words in the box with the correct form of *be going to*.

clean her room every weekend   check out the gym
give up eating French fries   start up a business
~~make some changes in their lives~~   take up running

1 Amy and her Dad *are going to make some changes in their lives* .

2 Dad _____ .

3 Amy _____ .

4 Mom and Dad _____ .

5 Amy _____ .

6 **Dad:** _____ you and Jodie _____ ?
   Amy: Yes, we _____ .

✱ be going to: predictions

c Read the rule. Then complete the sentences with *be going to* and the verb in parentheses.

RULE: We also use *be going to* to make predictions based on what we know or can see (for example, *I think it's going to be an interesting year.*).

1 There isn't a cloud in the sky. It *'s going to be* (be) sunny tomorrow.

2 The river is deep here. It _____ (not be) easy to get across.

3 I know they like modern art. They _____ (love) this painting.

4 It's 8:40, Steve! You _____ (be) late!

5 Angela _____ (not get) good grades this year. She hardly ever studies at home.

6 _____ we _____ (win) the game?

d Match the sentences with the pictures. Write 1–6 in the boxes.

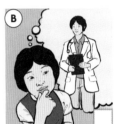

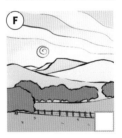

1 He's going to swim.

2 I'm going to cook a great meal tonight!

3 It's going to be a beautiful day.

4 They aren't going to eat anything else today!

5 Mom's going to be angry!

6 I'm going to be a doctor when I grow up.

e Which of the sentences in Exercise 4d are intentions? Which are predictions?

5 Pronunciation

▶ **CD2 T29** Pronunciation section starts on page 114.

6 Speak

a Work with a partner. Together, think of three changes you want to make to your town/city. Write them down.

b Work with someone from another pair. Tell each other what you decided with your first partner.

We're going to put bicycle lanes in ....
There's going to be a new mall in ....

7 Read and Listen

a Kate and Josh are going to a New Year's Eve party. Look at the first picture. Their parents are talking to them before they go. What do you think their parents are saying?

b ▶ **CD2 T30** Listen to Kate and Josh talking to their parents. Complete the dialogue. Check your ideas.

Kate: Mom? Dad? We're going now, OK?

Mom: OK, you two. Have a good time. But
¹ ....

Josh: Yes, Mom, we know.

Dad: You ² .... be home at 12:30.

Mom: You can stay at the party for the midnight celebration, but you ³ .... stay longer than that.

Kate: OK – no problem.

Josh: It isn't far, so we're ⁴ .... to leave at 12:15 and ⁵ .... back. We'll be home at 12:30.

Dad: Fine. Do you have your cell phones?

Mom: Yes, you can't ⁶ .... those.

Kate: We have mine. Josh lost his last week, remember?

Mom: OK. Call us if there's any problem, OK?

Josh: We will – ⁷ ....

Dad: OK – You'd better get going. Have a good time!

Kate: Thanks. See you later – I ⁸ .... , at 12:30.

c Look at the second picture. What do you think their parents are going to say?

d ▶ **CD2 T31** Why do you think they're home late? Listen and check your ideas.

e ▶ **CD2 T31** Put the sentences in the correct order. Listen again and check.

The police came and asked them questions. ☐

They waited with the woman. ☐

They called for an ambulance. ☐

The ambulance came. ☐

They left the party. ☐

They saw an accident. ☐

8 Grammar

✳ must/can't

a Look at the examples. Then complete the rule and the table.

*You **must** be home at 12:30.*

*You **can't** stay longer than that.*

RULE: We use _____ when we want to say that it's important to do something. We use _____ when we want to say that it's important *not* to do something.

Affirmative	Negative
I/you/we/they/he/she/ it _____ go	I/you/we/they/he/she/it _____ (**can not**) go

b Look at the pictures and complete the sentences. Use *must* or *can't* and a verb from the box.

stop   listen to   look   touch   ~~be~~   miss

1 I __*can't be*__ late for school!

2 I _____ for another job!

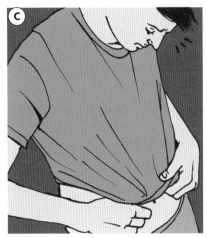

3 I _____ eating fried food!

DO NOT TOUCH

4 You _____ it!

5 Hurry! We _____ the beginning of the movie!

6 You _____ this CD. It's great!

LOOK!

You **don't have to leave** = You can leave if you want to, but it isn't obligatory.
You **can't leave** = You are not allowed to leave.

Culture in mind

9 Read and listen

a Do you listen to music at these times? Write *Y* (yes) or *N* (no). Then compare with a partner.

when you're doing homework ☐

when you wake up in the morning ☐

when you're walking along the street ☐

when you're feeling sad ☐

when you're feeling happy ☐

when you're eating ☐

b ▶ CD2 T32 Read the text and listen. Answer the questions below.

1 When did reggae become popular?

2 What type of music did reggae develop from?

3 How is reggae different from rock music?

4 What did Jimmy Cliff combine?

5 Who did Bob Marley play with originally?

10 Vocabulary

* Prepositions

a Complete the sentences with the correct preposition.

1 Music these days is very different ___*from*___ 20 years ago.

2 When I hear this song, I always think _____ our last vacation.

3 Rap is not similar _____ reggae.

4 Do you believe _____ the power of music to make you feel happy or sad?

5 A lot of rock music developed _____ rhythm and blues.

6 This is a great song! I'm sure it'll go _____ the charts soon.

b (Circle) the correct word.

1 For me, the (rhythm) / reggae of a piece of music is what's important.

2 Madonna is still making *miss / hit* records after all this time.

3 Look at the music *charts / pops* to find out what CD you should buy Emily.

4 What's more important, the music or the *blues / lyrics*?

5 The *style / combination* of bass guitar and drums can sound great!

6 We all believe *same / equal* rights are important, don't we?

Reggae music

Reggae music became a popular musical style more than 50 years ago. When people hear the word "reggae," they usually think of Jamaica, but in fact, reggae developed in New Orleans in the U.S., from a type of music called rhythm and blues (R and B). Musicians changed the beat of R and B and rock music and made a new musical style. It was the beginning of reggae.

Some people say that the reggae beat is similar to the rhythm of the human heartbeat.

It's different from rock music, and is generally easier to sing and dance to. In the 1960s, a lot of young black people wanted to use reggae songs to fight for political freedom and equal rights. For them, the lyrics were very important. But other people wanted reggae to be simply "good music." Jimmy Cliff, with his song "Wonderful World, Beautiful People," was the first person to really bring together reggae music and the "peace and love" ideas that the hippies of the 1960s believed in.

In the 1960s and the 1970s, there were many reggae bands on the music charts. One of the most famous was the Wailers (Bob Marley, Peter Tosh and Bunny Wailer). Tosh and Wailer left the group, but Bob Marley continued to make hit songs like "I Shot the Sheriff," and he became the most famous reggae musician of all time. He died very young, at the age of 36.

11 Listen: a song

▶ **CD2 T33** Complete the Jimmy Cliff song with the words in the box. Then listen and check your answers.

love free helping world secret pretty

Wonderful World, Beautiful People

[Chorus]
Wonderful world, beautiful people
You and your girl, things could be ¹ ....
But underneath this there is a ² ....
That nobody can repeat.

Take a look at the ³ .... **and the state**
that it's in today
I am sure you'll agree we all could make it
a better way
With our ⁴ .... **put together everybody**
learn to love each other
Instead of fussing and fighting, cheating
back biting
Scandalizing and hating.
Baby we could have a ...

[Chorus]

Man and woman, girl and boy, let us try
to give a ⁵ .... **hand**
This I know and I'm sure that the love we
all could understand
This is our world, can't you see
Everybody wants to live and be ⁶ ....
Instead of fussing and fighting, cheating
back biting
Scandalizing and hating.
Yeah, we could have a...

[Chorus]

12 Speak

Discuss in class.

1 What is the singer worried about?

2 What kind of "better way" does he want for the world?

3 Do you think that the lyrics of a song are important or just the music?

13 Write

Imagine it's January 1 and you get this email from your American friend, Jessie.

Hi, (your name)!

Happy New Year! How are you? Did you have a good time last night?

We only had a small party here at home, just my family and a few friends. But it was OK, and I didn't go to bed until 2:00 in the morning.

This email is part of my New Year's resolution. I'm going to write a lot more emails this year! My dad says he's going to quit eating junk food and go running every morning. He said this last year, but he soon broke his resolution. Do you have any resolutions for this year?

We're on vacation this week, so I'm going to relax and spend some time with my friends. It snowed here yesterday, so we're going to do some snowboarding.

Write soon!

Bye for now,

Jessie

Write an email reply to Jessie. Tell her about:

● your New Year's Eve

● your New Year's resolution(s) and a resolution made by someone in your family

● what you're going to do this week

For your portfolio

✳ First conditional; *when* and *if*
✳ Vocabulary: adjectives of feeling

1 Read and listen

a Look at the pictures. What do you think the text is about?

1 A man who didn't feel well on the platform of a New York subway station.

2 A man who saved another man in the New York subway.

3 The man who designed the platforms of the New York subway.

Read the text quickly and check your answer.

b ▶ CD2 T34   Now read the text again and listen. Answer the questions.

1 Why did Mr. Hollopeter fall onto the platform and then the track?

2 How deep was the space where Mr. Hollopeter fell?

3 Why did five subway cars travel over the two men?

4 Who was Mr. Autrey worried about when the train stopped?

5 What was the only thing that happened to Mr. Autrey?

Subway hero

It was 12:45 p.m. on January 2, 2007. Fifty-year-old Wesley Autrey was waiting for the train at a subway station in New York. His two daughters, ages four and six, were with him.

Suddenly, a sick man collapsed on the platform. The man, 20-year-old Cameron Hollopeter, got up, but then fell again – this time, onto the track between the two rails. A train was coming into the station. It was a frightening moment.

But Mr. Autrey wasn't frightened. He looked at the man, and he looked at the space that the man was in. It was about half a meter deep. And he thought, "The train is going to travel over this man. If he tries to get up, the train will kill him. But if he lies on the ground and doesn't move, he'll be OK." So he knew he had to make a decision.

He jumped. Mr. Autrey lay on top of Mr. Hollopeter, and kept him down on the ground. The train driver saw them. He was terrified, but he couldn't stop in time. Five subway cars traveled over the two men before the train stopped.

The people on the platform were shocked. When Mr. Autrey heard them screaming, he shouted, "We're OK down here, but I have two daughters up there. Let them know their father's OK." People on the platform clapped and cheered. They were amazed at Mr. Autrey's courage. Subway workers helped the two men out. An ambulance took Mr. Hollopeter to the hospital. He had no serious injuries.

In an interview on a TV show, Mr. Autrey said, "The only thing that happened to me was my blue hat got dirty."

He added, "I wasn't brave. I didn't do anything special. I just saw someone who needed help. I did what I thought was right."

c Do you think Mr. Autrey was brave?

d Find words and phrases in the text on page 92 with these meanings.

1 fell down because he was sick (paragraph 2)

2 make a choice about what to do after thinking about several possibilities (paragraph 3)

3 put their hands together to say "Good job" (paragraph 5)

4 damage to someone's body because of an accident (paragraph 5)

e Tell the class about a time when you were brave.

2 Grammar

✳ First conditional

a Match the two halves of the sentences. Check by looking back at the text on page 92.

1 If he tries to get up,   a he'll be OK.

2 If he doesn't move,   b the train will kill him.

b Read the rule and complete the table.

> **RULE:** We use the first conditional to talk about things we think are possible in the future.

If clause	Result clause
If + simple present	.... (will) .... (will not) + base form

c Put the words into the correct order to make sentences.

1 see Jane / if / tell / I / I'll / her

----

2 my parents / I'm / will / if / late / be angry

----

3 I / bring it / I'll / to school tomorrow / if / remember

----

4 you'll / new friend, Jake / come / if / you / meet / my / to the party

----

5 rain tomorrow / if / the / it / doesn't / we'll / to / beach / go

----

d Complete the first conditional sentences with the correct form of the verbs.

1 If Kate ___helps___ (help) me, I ___'ll finish___ (finish) my homework in an hour.

2 You _____ (not meet) anyone if you _____ (not go out).

3 I _____ (come) to your party if my mom _____ (say) I can.

4 If Danilo _____ (not want) his ice cream, I _____ (eat) it.

5 Susan _____ (be) angry if she _____ (hear) about this.

6 If we _____ (buy) hamburgers, we _____ (not have) enough money for the movie.

3 Speak

Work with a partner.

Student A: Look at the questions below.

Student B: Turn to page 117.

Ask your questions and answer your partner's.

Student A

1 What will you do if it rains this weekend?

2 What will you do if the weather's nice?

3 How will you feel if your teacher gives you a lot of homework today?

4 What will you do if you're sick tomorrow?

5 What movie will you see if you go to the movies this week?

6 What show will you watch if you watch TV this evening?

4 Pronunciation

▶ **CD2 T35** Pronunciation section starts on page 114.

5 Grammar

✱ *when* and *if*

a What is the difference between sentences 1 and 2? Which speaker is sure he will see John?

1   *I'll give John your message when I see him.*
2   *I'll give John your message if I see him.*

b Complete the sentences with *if* or *when*.

1   I'm seeing Marta tomorrow. I'll ask her about the book
    ___when___ I meet her.

2   A: What are you doing tomorrow?

    B: _____ there's a good movie, I'll probably go see it.

3   I'm not sure if I want to go to the dance club tonight.
    But _____ I decide to go, I'll call you.

4   It's too hot out in the sun now. Let's play tennis in the evening,
    _____ it's cooler.

6 Vocabulary

✱ Adjectives of feeling

a Look at the examples from the text on page 92. Which adjective describes how the man felt? Which adjective describes the situation?

*It was a **frightening** moment.*
*But Mr. Autrey wasn't **frightened**.*

b <u>Underline</u> three more examples of *-ed* adjectives in the text on page 92.

c ▶ CD2 T36 Write the adjectives under the pictures. Then listen, check and repeat.

    tired   bored   ~~excited~~   interested   annoyed   frightened

d (Circle) the correct adjective in each sentence.

1   I didn't like the movie. I thought it was (boring) / bored.

2   It was a *terrifying / terrified* experience to lose my passport on vacation in a foreign country.

3   My friend, Flena, is really *scaring / scared* of spiders. She can't stand them!

4   The football game was really *exciting / excited*. In the end, the Bears won 3–2.

5   The class wasn't very *interesting / interested*, so some of the students almost fell asleep.

6   When we saw the news report about the bank robbery, we were really *shocked / shocking*.

7   My teacher was very *annoying / annoyed* when I told him I didn't have my homework.

8   I found the marathon really *tiring / tired*. I slept for 12 hours the next day!

excited

7 Listen and speak

a Look at the pictures. Use a word from each box to label the jobs.

| airline   dog   window   steel   ~~X-ray~~ | worker   trainer   washer   ~~assistant~~   pilot |

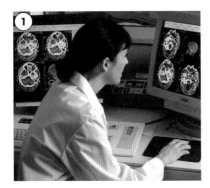

(1)

X-ray assistant

(2)

_____

(3)

_____

(4)

_____

(5)

_____

b Which words can go with each picture? Write the words in the lists.

Nouns:
~~X-rays~~   temperatures   ~~hospital~~   lift
animals   rope   passengers   fire
airport   teeth

Verbs:
~~make sick~~   land   bite   burn   fall

Picture 1 __X-rays__ _____ __hospital__ _____ __make sick__

Picture 2 _____ _____ _____

Picture 3 _____ _____ _____

Picture 4 _____ _____ _____

Picture 5 _____ _____ _____

c How brave do you think the people are? For each picture in Exercise 7a, write a score of 1–5.

(1 = not very brave, 5 = extremely brave)

Picture 1 _____   Picture 4 _____

Picture 2 _____   Picture 5 _____

Picture 3 _____

d ▶ **CD2 T37** Listen to Tony and Claudia. Which three pictures are they talking about? Complete the first column of the table.

	Tony	Claudia
Picture _3_	_4_	_____
Picture ___	___	_____
Picture ___	___	_____

e ▶ **CD2 T37** Listen again. Write the scores that Tony and Claudia give to each person.

f Work with a partner. Talk about the scores you gave in Exercise 7c.

A: _What score did you give to the dog trainer? I gave her a three. I don't think you have to be brave to work with dogs._

B: _I don't agree. I gave her five points because ..._

Chicken

a Look at the photostory. Kim is angry because Matt calls her "chicken." What do you think he means? Read and listen to find the answer.

①

Ms. H: Kim? The people at Star Senior Center – you know, the activity center for older people – want someone to give a presentation. Could you do it?

Kim: Me? Stand up and talk? I can't do that!

Ms. H: Yes, you can. It's not a big deal.

②

Emily: You told Ms. H. no? Why? The people at the senior center aren't going to laugh or be mean.

Kim: I know. But ... oh, I don't know. I'm just not brave enough, that's all. I can't do it, and that's that.

③

Emily: Here she comes. Go ahead, Matt.

Matt: Hey, look, Emily. Kim's the school chicken! *Bawk! Bawk!*

Kim: Excuse me?

Matt: I hear you won't give a presentation at the senior center. Ooh, the people there are so scary! Pathetic!

Kim: Chicken? Pathetic? No one calls me that!

④

Kim: Ms. Harrison? I changed my mind. I want to do that presentation after all.

Ms. H: Good for you, Kim. How about Friday, around 1:00?

......

Emily: It worked! Good job, Matt.

Matt: Thanks. But I don't think Kim will ever talk to me again!

b Mark the statements *T* (true) or *F* (false).

1 The people at Star Senior Center want Kim to give a presentation. [*T*]

2 At first, Kim doesn't want to give a presentation. ☐

3 Emily tells Kim that she's not brave. ☐

4 Kim thinks the people will laugh at her. ☐

5 Matt tells Kim that she's not brave. ☐

6 Kim is very angry. ☐

7 Later, Kim tells Ms. Harrison that she wants to do the presentation. ☐

8 Emily is happy that Matt did what she wanted him to do. ☐

9 Everyday English

a Find expressions 1–6 in the photostory. Who says them? How do you say them in your language?

1. ...not a big deal
2. ...and that's that
3. Go ahead.
4. Excuse me?
5. ... after all
6. Good job.

b Read the dialogues. Use the expressions in Exercise 9a to complete them.

1. A: Jenny, please come to the movies with me!

   B: Listen, Mark. I don't want to go to the movies with you, [1] *and that's that* . OK?

2. A: How did it go at the dentist's today?

   B: It was OK. I was really scared before I went, but it wasn't too bad [2] ....

3. A: That dress looks horrible!

   B: [3] .... ?

4. A: I heard that you won a skateboarding competition. [4] .... !

   B: Thanks. But it's [5] .... I mean, it was only a small competition.

5. A: I think the water's really cold. I don't want to go in!

   B: [6] .... ! It's OK. It's not *that* cold!

Discussion box

1. Why does Emily say, "It worked. Good job." to Matt?
2. How does Matt feel about the situation?
3. In what kind of situation do you feel you "can't do it"? Would it help if someone called you "chicken"? Why (not)?

---

10 Improvisation

Work with a partner. Take two minutes to prepare a short role play. Try to use some of the expressions from Exercise 9a. Do not write the text, just agree on your ideas for a short scene. Then act it out.

Roles: Kim and Matt

Situation: At school, a few hours later

Basic idea: Matt sees that Kim doesn't want to talk to him.

Use one of these sentences to start the conversation:

Kim: Hey, Matt. Can I talk to you?

Matt: Look, it's Kim. The school chicken!

11 Reach Out ⊙ DVD Episode 7

a Match the words and phrases with their definitions.

1. accident
2. computer lab
3. projector
4. bulb
5. responsibility
6. permission
7. fault

a. a machine that shows movies or images on a screen or wall
b. responsibility for doing something wrong
c. something that happens by mistake
d. a glass object that produces light
e. something that is your job or duty to deal with
f. if you are given ... to do something, you are allowed to do it
g. a computer room

b How does Alex feel? Work with a partner and make a story to explain. Then watch Episode 7 and find out what really happened.

12 Write

a Read what Geraldine wrote about a book she read. Answer the questions.

1 What was the book?

2 Who was the main character?

3 Where was he/she?

4 Why was he/she in danger?

5 What did he/she do?

6 How did the story end?

The book I read is *A Picture to Remember* by Sarah Scott-Malden.

It's about a girl called Christina. One day, she saw two men in a car. One of them had a gun. They were bank robbers, and she saw their faces. They didn't want her to tell the police, so they planned to kill her.

First, one of the robbers attacked her at the gym, but luckily, she only hurt her arm. After this, she was on the street with her friend, Philippe, when one of the robbers drove his car into them. Philippe was hurt and had to go to the hospital.

Christina went to visit Philippe. When she left the hospital in her friend's car, the robbers followed her. Christina saw that they had a gun and understood that they wanted to kill her. She was frightened, but she stayed calm. The robbers were close behind her, but they were driving too fast and couldn't stop. They crashed their car, and it overturned. Then the police caught both the robbers.

b Write about a movie, book or TV show where somebody was in a dangerous situation. Use the questions and Geraldine's text to help you.

13 Last but not least: more speaking

a Work alone. Think of a situation you know of when somebody was very brave / not very brave. Take a few minutes to think about the following questions.

- Where was it?
- Who were the people involved?
- What happened? Why was it important for someone to be brave?
- How did you feel in the situation?
- How did the situation end?

b Do a simple drawing of the situation. Here's an example:

c Now work with a partner. Show your partner your drawing. Your partner has ten questions to find out what happened. The questions need to be Yes/No questions.

A: *Did the person in the picture go down the stairs?*

B: *Yes.*

A: *Was it during the night?*

B: *No.*

d If your partner can't guess what happened and has asked all ten questions, tell him or her about the situation.

Check your progress

1 Grammar

a Complete the sentences. Use the verbs in the box with the correct form of *be going to*.

> visit   help   ~~rain~~   dance   wear
> not ride   not watch

1 Look at those clouds. It*'s going to rain* .
2 I have a difficult history project to do. My sister .... me with it.
3 I .... television tonight. All the shows are boring!
4 .... you .... your black jeans tonight?
5 My parents .... my grandfather this weekend.
6 Peter doesn't like horses. He .... with us this afternoon.
7 There's a party next Friday night, and we .... all night! | 6 |

b Complete each sentence with *must* or *can't*.

1 Come on, Julie! We ....*can't*.... be late!
2 It's a great book. You really .... read it.
3 Sorry, Jimmy, I'm late. I .... go now.
4 You .... tell anyone about this! It's too embarrassing.
5 Turn off your cell phone, Dee. You .... have it on in class.
6 I can go out with you tonight, but I .... be home before midnight.
7 OK, you can have a pet snake, but it .... come into the house! | 6 |

c Complete the first conditional sentences with the correct form of the verbs.

1 If you ....*help*.... (help) me, I .... (buy) you some ice cream.
2 If Jack .... (come) to school late, the teacher .... (be) really angry.
3 The neighbors .... (complain) if we .... (make) a lot of noise.
4 If I .... (have) time, I .... (get) the tickets this afternoon. | 7 |

2 Vocabulary

a Complete the sentences using the correct multi-word verbs.

1 We're all worried about his health. He should really ....*give up*.... junk food.
2 If you want to be fit, why don't you .... a sport?
3 If you don't understand this word, ... it .... in a dictionary.
4 The city had to .... the New Year's celebration because of rain.
5 You don't need to help me with this problem. I think I can .... it .... myself.
6 My uncle is a designer. He wants to .... his own business soon.
7 There's a new youth club on our street. Let's .... it .... | 6 |

b Complete the adjectives with the *-ed* or *-ing* ending.

1 I was really tir*ed* last night when I went to bed. Yesterday was a very tir........ day.
2 We were excit........ about going to the basketball game, but in the end, it was a bor........ game.
3 I thought the Dracula movie was really frighten........ , but my girlfriend wasn't frighten........ at all.
4 We went to a museum last Sunday. My parents thought it was really interest........ , but I was a little bor........ . | 7 |

How did you do?

Check your score.

Total score	☺	☹	☹
32	Very good	OK	Not very good
Grammar	19 – 15	14 – 12	11 or less
Vocabulary	13 – 11	10 – 8	7 or less

* *should/shouldn't; What's it like?*
* Vocabulary: personality adjectives, adjectives for expressing opinions

1 Read and listen

a Check that you know the meaning of these words. Match them with the pictures.

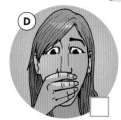

1 line
2 bump into
3 bus stop
4 shake hands
5 tip
6 cover your mouth

b ▶ CD2 T39 Listen to two people talking about mistakes they made when meeting people from other countries. Make notes to answer the questions:

1 Who are the other people involved?
2 What mistake(s) did the speaker or other people make in each situation?

c Have you ever made a similar mistake? Where were you? Who were you with? What happened?

d Read the questions in the quiz. What do you think? Write *T* (true) or *F* (false).

e ▶ CD2 T40 Listen and check your answers.

Quiz: What do you know about U.S. culture?

1 If you bump into someone, even by accident, you should say sorry. ☐

2 You should go to the front of the line at a bus stop or ticket booth. ☐

3 You shouldn't send text messages at a movie. ☐

4 When you meet someone, you should shake hands with your left hand. ☐

5 If someone invites you to dinner, you shouldn't arrive early. ☐

6 You shouldn't talk with food in your mouth. ☐

2 Grammar

★ should/shouldn't

a Look at the examples and read the rule. <u>Underline</u> examples of *should* and *shouldn't* in the quiz.

*You **should** say sorry.*
*You **shouldn't** talk if you have food in your mouth.*

> **RULE:** We use *should* or *shouldn't* to say "It's a good idea" or "It isn't a good idea."

b Complete the table.

Affirmative	Negative	Questions	Short answers
I/you/we/they/he/she/it **should** go	I/you/we/they/he/she/it .... (should not) go	Should/I/you/we/they/he/she/it go?	Yes, I/you/we/they/he/she/it .... No, you/we/they/he/she/it .... (should not).

c Complete the dialogues. Use *should* or *shouldn't* and a verb from the box.

go   watch   wear

1   **Steve:** I don't know which jacket to wear.
    Paul: The white one's great. I think you
    should wear that one.

2   **Julia:** There's a show about Japan on TV tonight.
    Tim: Really? Then I .... it. I'm doing a
    project on Japan.

3   **Alex:** My eyes really hurt. .... I ....
    to the doctor?
    Father: No, but you .... television so
    much, Alex.

4   **Amy:** I'm tired.
    Lucy: Me, too. It's almost 11:30. I think we
    .... to bed.

5   **Anna:** What do you think? I
    .... jeans to the party this evening?
    Carol: No, everybody's wearing dressy clothes.
    You .... your long dress.

6   **Hiro:** Mom, I feel awful this morning.
    Mother: Yes, you look sick. Maybe you
    .... to school today.

7   **You should always cover your mouth with your hand when you laugh.** ☐

8   **You shouldn't start eating until everyone at the table has their food.** ☐

9   **You shouldn't give waiters tips at restaurants.** ☐

HA-HA-HA!

3 Speak

Work with a partner.
Student A: Read the role card below.
Student B: Turn to page 117 and read the role card.
Take turns listening to your partner's problem and give advice with *should* or *shouldn't*.

> **Student A**
>
> You play the guitar in a band. You practice for about two hours every evening, so you don't have time to do all your schoolwork. Your parents are annoyed because your grades are bad. They want you to leave the band and do your schoolwork. You are very unhappy because you love playing in the band, but you want to get good grades in school, too. Should you stay in the band? Should you leave? Ask Student B.

4 Vocabulary

✱ Personality adjectives

a ▶ **CD2 T41** Listen and repeat the adjectives. Check that you understand their meaning.

> kind   hard-working   polite   honest   organized   ~~happy~~   relaxed   friendly

b Complete the sentences with the adjectives in Exercise 4a.

1   A __happy__ person usually smiles a lot.
2   An _____ person tells you what he/she really thinks.
3   A _____ person doesn't worry about things.
4   A _____ person works a lot.
5   An _____ person is neat and keeps things in order.

6   A _____ person helps people and thinks about their feelings.
7   A _____ person is easy to talk to and makes friends easily.
8   A _____ person always says *please* and *thank you*.

c ▶ **CD2 T42** Write the adjectives under the pictures. Then listen, check and repeat.

> unfriendly   dishonest   mean   lazy   miserable   nervous   rude   disorganized

A
B
C
D

E
F
G
H

d Complete the table of opposites.

Adjectives	Opposites
1 kind	_____mean_____
2 happy	_____
3 polite	_____
4 honest	_____
5 organized	_____
6 relaxed	_____
7 hard-working	_____
8 friendly	_____

e Complete the sentences with adjectives. Use your own ideas.

1   I think I'm a/an _____ person.
2   My best friend is _____ and _____ .
3   Our neighbors are very _____ .
4   I don't like people who are _____ .

5 Pronunciation

▶ **CD2 T43 and T44** Pronunciation section starts on page 114.

6 Grammar

✱ *What's it like?*

a Match the questions with the answers.

1 What was the weather like on your vacation? `d`

2 What's your new teacher like? ☐

3 What are the people like in New York? ☐

4 What was the movie like last night? ☐

5 What's this CD like? ☐

a They're very friendly and helpful.

b It's great! You should listen to it.

c Well, I thought it was a little boring.

d Awful! It rained all the time.

e She's nice, and she's really funny!

b When we ask for an opinion about something or someone, we can ask: *What + be + subject + like?* Look at the questions in Exercise 6a and complete the table.

What	is	he / .... / it	
	--------		.... ?
	--------	they	
	were		

c Write the questions. Use the words in parentheses.

1 A: I went to Greece last year.
   B: Really? What _was it like_ ? (it)

2 A: I got the new Mariah Carey CD.
   B: Oh? What _____ ? (it)

3 A: There's a new girl in our class.
   B: A new girl? What _____ ? (she)

4 A: We visited Spain a few weeks ago.
   B: Oh, that's nice! What _____ ? (the weather)

5 A: I got some new shoes.
   B: Really? What _____ ? (they)

6 A: I read three books last week.
   B: Wow! What _____ ? (they)

7 Vocabulary

✱ Adjectives for expressing opinions

a ▶ **CD2 T45** Here are some adjectives we can use to give an opinion. Write them in the columns. Then listen, check and repeat.

> ~~boring~~ ~~excellent~~ interesting attractive
> fantastic awful cool dull ugly horrible

+ (affirmative)	– (negative)
excellent	*boring*

b Which adjectives from Exercise 7a can you use to describe:

1 a movie?   3 a city/town?   5 the weather?

2 a person?   4 a party?

8 Speak

a Work with a partner. Ask and answer questions about the things in the box.

> your brother/sister/parents/boyfriend/girlfriend
> your town or city   your home   your last vacation
> your favorite singer   your last weekend

A: *What's your brother like?*

B: *He's OK sometimes. He's ____ .*

b Work with a different partner.

Student A has 1 minute to think of as many different questions as possible using "*What's ... like?*" Student A asks Student B the questions. Student B listens but doesn't answer.

Then Student B has one minute to remember the questions and answer them. He/She thinks of one "wrong" answer. When Student B finishes, Student A guesses the wrong answer.

Culture in mind

9 Read and listen

a Look at the text quickly and find answers to the following questions.

1 Who is the man in the picture?
2 What's his job?
3 Where is he from?

b ▶ CD2 T46 Read and listen to the text and check your answers.

c Find words in the text that mean:

1 the line on a map that separates two countries (paragraph 2)
2 a place where people live, smaller than a town (paragraph 2)
3 with no shoes on (paragraph 3)
4 an international soccer competition (paragraph 4)
5 in another country (paragraph 5)
6 the situation of being very poor (paragraph 5)

Heroic Ulises on a journey of hope

Tourists go to Ecuador to go whale or bird watching, to visit the Amazon rain forest, or to go to the Galápagos Islands, one of the world's most famous nature paradises.

But not many tourists go to the village of Piquiucho in the Chota Valley. It is near the Colombian border, about a three-hour drive north of the capital, Quito. Life for people in this village is hard, and many of them have simple huts for houses. But there's something very special about Piquiucho: Half of the soccer players who played for Ecuador in the World Cup in 2002 and 2006 (a total of 11 players) came from this poor village.

Piquiucho was the starting point for one man's journey of hope. Ulises de la Cruz started to play soccer barefoot as a child. His dream was to become a professional soccer player. And one day his dream came true. He played for his national team, and later in the English Premier League.

He earned a lot of money, but he didn't spend his money on fast cars and big houses. When Ecuador reached the World Cup finals in 2002, Ulises used the money he earned to buy a fresh water supply for Piquiucho. He used the money he made from playing for Ecuador in the 2006 World Cup to help the people of his village, too. "The 2006 World Cup in Germany was fantastic because it meant I could give money for a new sports and community center," he said.

10 Speak

Discuss in groups.

1. Which facts about Ecuador are new to you? Which ones did you already know?
2. What is your reaction to the story about Ulises de la Cruz?
3. Do you think what he does is "heroic"? Why / why not?

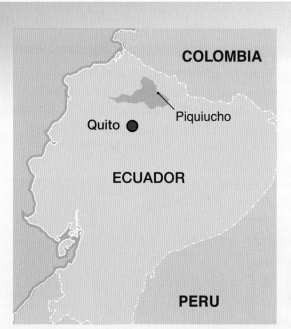

COLOMBIA

Piquiucho

Quito ●

ECUADOR

PERU

He pays for breakfast and lunch for 100 school children every day. Since he started to play abroad, he has sent hundreds of thousands of dollars back to his village. He has set up a medical center there, and he pays for a doctor, a dentist and a nurse. "I want to help the children of Piquiucho. I want to show them that they have a better future. I want to show them that by studying, they can help themselves to escape poverty. Soccer isn't the only way out."

11 Write

a Brianna's e-pal Carla is visiting the U.S. in March. Read Brianna's email and match the topics with the paragraphs.

a Things that Carla should/shouldn't do in the U.S. ☐

b Things that Carla should take to the U.S. ☐

c American people. ☐

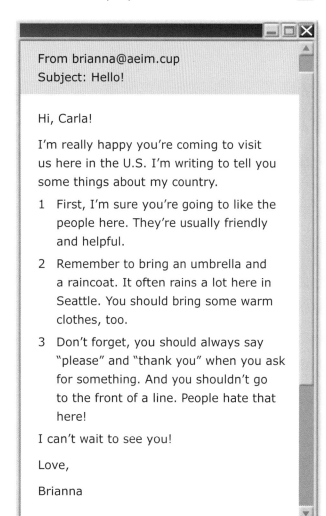

From brianna@aeim.cup
Subject: Hello!

Hi, Carla!

I'm really happy you're coming to visit us here in the U.S. I'm writing to tell you some things about my country.

1. First, I'm sure you're going to like the people here. They're usually friendly and helpful.

2. Remember to bring an umbrella and a raincoat. It often rains a lot here in Seattle. You should bring some warm clothes, too.

3. Don't forget, you should always say "please" and "thank you" when you ask for something. And you shouldn't go to the front of a line. People hate that here!

I can't wait to see you!

Love,

Brianna

b Work with a partner. Make a list of useful tips for American tourists who are coming to visit your country.

c Imagine that your English-speaking e-pal is visiting your country soon. Write a similar email to him/her.

* Present perfect + *ever/never*
* Vocabulary: verb and noun pairs, expressions about sleep

1 Read and listen

a Read the texts quickly. Match them with the pictures.

b ▶ CD3 T02 One of the texts has facts that are incorrect. Read the text again and listen. Correct the facts.

c What do you think about these records? Tell others in your class.

You've never seen anything like this!

People do some unusual things, and some of them have appeared in the record books. Here are a few examples. Have you ever seen anything as strange as this?

1 Saimir Strati from Albania built the largest picture ever made from toothpicks. The artist used 1.5 million toothpicks and worked 40 days to do it.

2 On February 2, 2004, 15,851 parents, students and teachers made snow angels at the same time in Ontario, Canada. It was the largest group of people that has ever come together to make snow angels.

3 Lee Redmond from the United States broke the world record for the longest fingernails in 1979. On February 23, 2008, her fingernails were a total length of 8.65 m long. Her longest nail is on her right thumb. It's 90 cm! Some people think she's never cut them!

4 The people at Miniature Wunderland in Hamburg, Germany, have constructed the longest model train in the world. It has 13 locomotives and 778 cars and measures 110 m! How long would a real train with this many locomotives and cars be? The answer: almost 1,000 km!

2 Grammar

✳ Present perfect + *ever/never*

a Look at the examples. Complete the rule and the table.

*Some people **have appeared** in the record books.*
***Have** you ever **seen** anything as strange as this?*
*She's **never** cut them!*

> **RULE:** We use the present perfect to talk about actions that happened some time up to now.
>
> We form the present perfect with the present tense of _____ + past participle.

Affirmative	Negative	Questions	Short answers
I/you/we/they 've (_*have*_) work**ed**	I/you/we/they (_____) (**have not**) work**ed**	_____ I/you/we/they work**ed**?	Yes, I/you/we/they **have**. No, I/you/we/they **haven't**.
he/she/it 's (_____) work**ed**	he/she/it **hasn't** (_____) work**ed**	_____ he/she/it work**ed**?	Yes, he/she/it **has**. No, he/she/it **hasn't**.

b Fill in the verb forms. Use the Irregular verbs list on page 122 to help you.

Base form	Past participle
1 be	*been*
2 do	_____
3 go	_____
4 see	_____
5 write	_____
6 bite	_____
7 speak	_____
8 eat	_____
9 drive	_____
10 fly	_____
11 swim	_____
12 win	_____

LOOK!

He **has gone** to New York.
= He is not here now –
he is in New York.

He **has been** to New York.
= At some time in the past,
he went to New York
and came back.

c Complete the sentences. Use the present perfect form of the verbs.

1 We _'ve never lived_ (never/live) in a foreign country.
2 I _____ _____ _____ (never/see) a tarantula.
3 _____ you _____ _____ (ever/drive) a car?
4 Sorry, Alena isn't here. She _____ _____ (go) to the movies.
5 Jack _____ _____ (be) to Japan, but he _____ _____ _____ (never/eat) sushi.

3 Pronunciation

▶ **CD3 T03** Pronunciation section starts on page 114.

4 Speak

a Work with a partner. Ask and answer the questions.

1 ever / see / a tiger?
2 ever / eat / Chinese food?
3 ever / be / on TV?
4 ever / speak / to a Brazilian person?
5 ever / win / any money?
6 ever / be / to Chicago?

A: *Have you ever seen a tiger?*
B: *No, never. Have you ever eaten Chinese food?*
A: *Yes, I have.*

b Work with a partner or in a small group. Ask and answer questions about things you have done in your life. Use some of the verbs in the box.

travel   stay   play   win   eat   fly   drive   meet

5 Vocabulary

✳ Verb and noun pairs

a Look at the examples of verb and noun pairs from the text in Exercise 1 on page 106.

*She has **broken the world record** for the longest fingernails.*

*He has **built the world's biggest motorcycle.***

Match the verbs with the nouns.

Verbs	Nouns
1 raise	a a risk
2 win	b a prize
3 break	c a joke
4 build	d a record
5 tell	e money
6 take	f a house

b Complete the sentences. Use verbs from Exercise 5a in the correct form.

1 In the 1968 Olympics long jump, Bob Beamon ___won___ the gold medal, and he _____ the world record.

2 Right now, Sandro's parents _____ _____ a new house.

3 The charity, Oxfam, _____ a lot of money every year for poor people.

4 Esra _____ a risk when she rode her bike without a helmet.

5 I like Steve because he _____ really good jokes.

c <u>Underline</u> the verb + noun combination in each sentence.

1 I'm tired now, so I think I'll <u>do</u> my <u>homework</u> tomorrow morning.

2 Sorry, he can't talk to you now, he's taking a shower.

3 My grandfather tells really good stories about when he was young.

4 My mom isn't feeling well, so I'm going to make dinner tonight.

5 Tonight I'm going to spend a little time with my friends.

6 My brother is taking a very important exam today.

6 Read

a Look at the pictures. Which one shows:

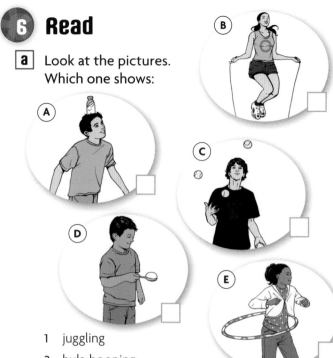

1 juggling

2 hula hooping

3 balancing a bottle on your head

4 jumping rope

5 balancing an egg on a spoon

b Read the text quickly. Which thing in Exercise 6a is not mentioned in the text?

He holds the record – for records!

Ashrita Furman has always been interested in Guinness World Records. As a teenager, he spent a lot of time reading the book, and today, he holds the most amazing record of all: The record for having the most current Guinness World Records at the same time! He has set 245 records since 1979. Other people broke some of his records, but today, he still holds 94 records.

Most of his records involve physical activity. For example, he has walked 103 kilometers while balancing a milk bottle on his head! It took him 23 hours and 35 minutes. He has also pushed a car just over 27 kilometers in 24 hours.

A few years ago, Furman set three new records in less than an hour on the same day. First, he ran a mile in 11 minutes and 12 seconds – while hula hooping. A few minutes later, he ran a mile balancing a raw egg on a spoon in 7 minutes and 47 seconds. And then he set a new record for jumping one mile on a pogo stick in 24 minutes and 49 seconds while juggling. These were Furman's 115th, 116th and 117th Guinness World Records. And he hasn't finished. Furman's life is all about breaking records, and by the time you read this, he's probably already broken a few more!

c Read the text again. Answer the questions.

1 How many records has Furman set?
2 How far has he walked with a bottle on his head?
3 How long did it take him to break three records on the same day?

7 Listen

a Which of these things do you think are the hardest to do? Discuss with a partner.

- not eat anything for three days
- not open your eyes for three days
- not sleep for three days
- not sit down for three days

b What do you think is the world record for not sleeping?

a 8 days   b 11 days

c 13 days   d 16 days

c ▶ CD3 T04 Listen to a conversation between Matthew and Grace. Check your answer to Exercise 7b.

d ▶ CD3 T04 Listen again and answer the questions.

1 What article have Matthew and Grace read?
2 What does Grace think about the person in the article?
3 What does Grace say Matthew does after 30 minutes at school?
4 What does Matthew say he does in class?
5 When did the American man set the world record for not sleeping?
6 How long did the American man sleep after he broke the record?

8 Vocabulary

✱ Expressions about sleep

a ▶ CD3 T05 Look at the expressions about sleep. Match the opposites. Then listen, check and repeat.

1 to go to bed   a to wake up
2 to go to sleep   b to be awake
3 to be asleep   c to get up

b What's the difference between *dreaming* and *daydreaming*?

c Complete the sentences with the expressions in the box. Use the correct form of the verbs. You can check the list of irregular verbs on page 122.

> wake up   go to sleep   ~~go to bed~~   be asleep
> get up   be awake   dream   daydream

1 My mother was very tired last night. She _went to bed_ at nine o'clock.
2 Sometimes I go to bed at ten. Then I read a book for an hour and I _____ at about eleven.
3 Last night Lucy _____ about winning the lottery.
4 Please talk quietly. The baby _____ .
5 I didn't sleep at all last night. I _____ all night.
6 This morning I _____ at six o'clock, but I'm lazy, so I stayed in bed and I _____ at eight.
7 Nick doesn't listen to the teacher. He _____ about being a famous singer.

9 Speak

a Complete each of these questions. Write one word in each space.

1 What time do you usually _go_ to bed during the week?
2 Do you sometimes read in bed before you go to _____ ?
3 What time do you usually get _____ during the week?
4 When you _____ up, do you usually get up immediately?
5 When you _____ , do you often remember it when you wake up?
6 Do you look out of the window and _____ ?

b Work with a partner. Ask and answer the questions.

What's next?

10 ▶ CD3 T06 **Read and listen**

a Look at the title. What do you think Emily, Kim, Alex and Matt are talking about? Read and listen to find the answer.

Kim: Do you know what I'm thinking?

Alex: No, what, Kim?

Kim: We should go to the café. We haven't been in a while.

Emily: Well, Matt and I went there a few weeks ago.

Matt: That's right. We did. Emily had a huge bowl of ice cream!

Emily: Hey, watch what you say, Matt!

Matt: Just joking, Emily! Tell you what, I'll pay today!

Alex: That's what I like to hear!

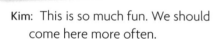

Kim: This is so much fun. We should come here more often.

Alex: Definitely!

Emily: By the way, what's the next assignment for English?

Matt: We have to talk about our hobbies.

Alex: Oh, yeah. What are you going to talk about, Matt?

Matt: Wait and see!

Alex: I'm going to talk about pet snakes, and I'm bringing my own pet snake to class!

Emily: Snakes? No, please, I hate them!

Matt: I think he's joking, Emily.

Kim: Oh, Alex, you're always joking around!

b Match. Then put the sentences in the correct order. Write 1–6 in the boxes.

a ☐ Emily changes the subject and asks   1 a pet snake, but he's only joking.

b ☐ Kim thinks   2 what their next English assignment is.

c ☐ Alex says he has   3 talk about their hobbies.

d ☐ Matt says they have to   4 to buy drinks for everyone.

e ☐ Matt doesn't tell them   5 they should go to the café again.

f ☐ Matt offers   6 what he's going to talk about.

11 Everyday English

a Find expressions 1–6 in the photostory. Who says them? How do you say them in your language?

1 … in a while.
2 Watch what you say.
3 Tell you what, …
4 Definitely!
5 By the way, …
6 Wait and see!

b Read the dialogues. Use the expressions in Exercise 11a to complete them.

1 A: What are you going to give me for my birthday?
   B: ¹ *Wait and see!*

2 A: I'm hungry.
   B: Me too. ² _____ , let's go to the café and get a sandwich.

3 A: I really like Sarah. Do you?
   B: ³ _____ ! She's really nice and tells great jokes, too.

4 A: Hi, Joe! I haven't seen you ⁴ _____ .
   B: I know. I was sick, but I'm better now.

5 A: Wow! This song's awful!
   B: ⁵ _____ ! This is my favorite band's new record!

6 A: That was a great party last night.
   B: It was really great! ⁶ _____ , I'm having a party next week. Do you want to come?

> ### Discussion box
> 1 In what situations do you enjoy laughing and making jokes with your friends?
> 2 How do you feel if someone jokes around <u>all</u> the time?

12 Improvisation

Work with a partner. Take two minutes to prepare a short role play. Try to use some of the expressions from Exercise 11a. Do not write the text, just agree on your ideas for a short scene. Then act it out.

Roles: Kim and Alex

Situation: They are on the phone a few hours later

Basic idea: Kim wants to play a joke on Alex. She has an idea and calls him.

Use one of these sentences to start the conversation:

Kim: Hi, Alex. Guess what?

Kim: Oh, Alex, I was wondering if you could help me with the assignment on hobbies.

13 Reach Out ⊙ DVD Episode 8

a What does the picture show?

a a karate class
b a dance class
c a qigong class
d a gymnastics class

b How do you think Kim feels about the class?

c Watch Episode 8 and find out.

14 Write

a Imagine you are staying with an American family in Los Angeles. You have received this email from an English-speaking friend. What topics does she ask about?

b Write an email or letter in reply to Louise. Start like this:

> Dear Louise,
>
> Thanks for your email and the photo. It was great to hear from you.
>
> I'm having a wonderful time here in Los Angeles.

> Dear (your name),
>
> How are you? Are you enjoying yourself in Los Angeles? I hope your trip there was OK, and you weren't too tired when you arrived.
>
> Please tell me all about the family you're staying with. What are they like? What have you done and seen in Los Angeles? Have you met any interesting people? Have you visited Hollywood and have you seen any movie stars?
>
> I'm having a good time. I've started horseback-riding classes, so I'm sending a photo of me on Fury, one of the horses at our riding school. I've also finished all my exams (great!), and my sister has passed her driving test, so now she can drive me everywhere!
>
> Write soon, OK?
>
> Love,
>
> Louise

15 Last but not least: more speaking

a Complete each of these sentences with something that is true for you. Use the pictures to help you with ideas.

1 I've never _____ , but I really want to ... !
2 I've never _____ , and I really don't want to ... !
3 I've never _____ , but I'm sure that I will in the future.
4 I've never _____ , and I don't think that I ever will.

b Work in pairs or groups. Tell other students about your sentences. Ask them about theirs.

A: *I've never been to New York City, but I really want to go one day!*

B: *Why do you want to go to New York?*

A: *I'm sure it's a really cool city.*

B: *OK. My turn. I've never touched a snake, and I don't think I ever will.*

A: *Why?*

B: *I think they're cool animals, but there aren't any snakes in this country!*

Check your progress

1 Grammar

a Complete the sentences with *should* or *shouldn't*.

1 You *shouldn't* eat a lot of fried food.

2 I _____ exercise more. I'd like to be in better shape.

3 When you wait for a movie in the U.S., you _____ stand in line.

4 They _____ get some exercise. They _____ spend so much time in front of the computer.

5 You look great! You _____ worry about losing weight!

6 Maria is feeling sick. _____ we take her to the doctor? ☐ 6

b Write sentences in the present perfect.

1 I / never / see / a tarantula.

   I've never seen a tarantula.

2 My brother / never / study / a foreign language.

   _____ .

3 My parents / never / fly / in a plane.

   _____ .

4 I / never / get / 100% on a test.

   _____ .

5 Richard / never / eat / frogs' legs.

   _____ .

6 your teacher / ever / shout / at you?

   _____ ?

7 you / ever / speak / to a Russian person?

   _____ ?

8 your parents / ever / win / a competition?

   _____ ? ☐ 7

2 Vocabulary

a Write the opposites of the adjectives.

1 honest   *dishonest*

2 kind   _____

3 organized   _____

4 happy   _____

5 friendly   _____

6 polite   _____

7 hard-working   _____

8 relaxed   _____ ☐ 7

b Complete the sentences with the correct verb from the box. Change the form when necessary.

> raise   build   spend
> ~~break~~   do   tell   take

1 He is a good runner, but he will never ___*break*___ a record.

2 At school we are trying to _____ money for a family whose house burned down.

3 Stop _____ jokes now. We really have other things to do.

4 It only took them three months to _____ the house.

5 I'm so hot. I'd like to _____ a shower.

6 He _____ hours watching TV every night. How boring!

7 Sorry, I don't have any time. I need to _____ my homework now. ☐ 6

How did you do?

Check your score.

Total score	☺	☺	☹
☐ 26	Very good	OK	Not very good
Grammar	13 – 11	10 – 8	7 or less
Vocabulary	13 – 11	10 – 8	7 or less

Phonetic symbols

Consonants

Phonetic symbol:	Key words:
/p/	purple, apple
/b/	bicycle, hobby
/t/	table, litter
/d/	different, ride
/k/	desk, computer
/g/	game, dog
/f/	fun, sofa, photo
/v/	vegetables, favorite
/m/	mother, some
/n/	nose, lawn, know
/ŋ/	English, long
/s/	sit, pencil
/z/	zero, those
/w/	wind, one
/l/	laundry, small
/r/	red, rare
/y/	your, usually
/h/	house, who
/θ/	three, math
/ð/	father, this
/ʃ/	shop, station
/ʒ/	television, garage
/tʃ/	chocolate, kitchen
/dʒ/	jump, damage

Vowels

Phonetic symbol:	Key words:
/æ/	bad, taxi
/ɑ/	stop, opera
/ɛ/	chess, bed
/ə/	dramatic, the
/ɪ/	dish, sit
/i/	real, screen
/ʊ/	good, full
/u/	choose, view
/ʌ/	must, done
/ɔ/	strawberry, daughter

Vowels + /r/

Phonetic symbol:	Key words:
/ər/	first, shirt
/ɑr/	car
/ɔr/	horse
/ɛr/	their
/ʊr/	tourist
/ɪr/	ear

Diphthongs

Phonetic symbol:	Key words:
/eɪ/	play, train
/aɪ/	ice, night
/ɔɪ/	employer, noisy
/aʊ/	house, download
/oʊ/	no, window

Unit 1 /h/ (have)

a ▶ CD1 T05 Listen and repeat the words.

/h/ how hi house here have has hair

b ▶ CD1 T06 Listen and repeat the sentences.

1 Ken has brown hair.
2 Hi, Jack. How are you?
3 Henry lives here. He lives in a big house.

Unit 2 can/can't

a ▶ CD1 T09 Listen to these sentences. Notice the pronunciation of *can* and *can't*. Listen and repeat.

1 Can you swim?
2 I can swim.
3 I can't swim.

b ▶ CD1 T10 Listen to the sentences. Circle the words you hear.

1 Olivia (*can / can't*) play the piano.
2 Phil (*can / can't*) draw.
3 (*Can / Can't*) they paint?
4 Rex and Martin (*can / can't*) speak Italian.

Unit 3 /n/ (ma<u>n</u>) and /ŋ/ (so<u>ng</u>)

a ▶ CD1 T17 Listen and repeat the words.

/n/ man fun town Japan listen Italian
/ŋ/ thing song sing morning writing

b ▶ CD1 T18 Listen and repeat the sentences.

1 Jenny likes dancing and painting.
2 Dan enjoys running in the morning.
3 We sing songs for fun.

Unit 4 /ər/ (w<u>or</u>ld)

a ▶ CD1 T21 Listen and repeat the words.

her world work learn birthday other

b ▶ CD1 T22 Listen and repeat the sentences.

1 They volunteer all over the world.
2 He always works hard.
3 Learn these words!
4 Do you know her other friends?

Unit 5 *was* and *were*

a ▶ **CD1 T28** Listen to the sentences. What vowel sound do you hear? Listen again and repeat.

1 Erin was an American woman.
2 There were a lot of papers on the table.
3 Was the water clean?
4 Were the people sick?

b ▶ **CD1 T29** Listen and check (✓) the vowel sound you hear. Then listen again and repeat.

	/ɑ/	/ər/
1 I was unhappy.	☐	☐
2 We were late yesterday.	☐	☐
3 Was it noisy?	☐	☐
4 Yes, it was.	☐	☐

-ed endings

c ▶ **CD1 T30** Listen to the sentences. Write the words in bold in the lists.

1 We **walked** a long way.
2 We **visited** an interesting museum.
3 I **used** a red pen to do the test.
4 We **wanted** another hamburger.
5 I **watched** a great movie last night.
6 My painting was awful, so I **started** again.

/d/ or /t/	/ɪd/
walked	*visited*

Unit 6 Word stress

a ▶ **CD1 T36** Look at the list. How many syllables does each word have? Listen and check.

1 surfing   3 sports   5 skateboarding
2 basketball   4 cycling   6 champion

b ▶ **CD1 T36** Write the words in the lists. Then listen again and check.

●　　　●●　　　●●●

Unit 7 *have to*

Usually, *have* has a /v/ sound, but in *have to / don't have to*, it has a /f/ sound. Also *to* has the weak sound /ə/.

▶ **CD1 T41** Listen and repeat the sentences.

1 I have to go.
2 You don't have to shout.
3 He doesn't have to come.
4 We have to learn English.

Unit 8 The schwa /ə/ (*the*)

a ▶ **CD1 T48** The most common vowel sound in English is /ə/. Listen and repeat.

breakfast   bacon   tomato   banana
diet   vegetable

b ▶ **CD1 T49** Listen and underline the syllables with the /ə/ sound. Then listen again and repeat.

a carrot   an orange   a lemon
some apples   some onions   a lot of fruit
a lot of potatoes   a lot of vegetables

Unit 9 *than*

a ▶ **CD2 T04** Listen to the sentences and underline the stressed syllables.

1 Pronunciation is more difficult than grammar.
2 Spanish is easier than German.
3 My speaking is better than my writing.
4 Is French more interesting than English?

b ▶ **CD2 T04** How do you pronounce *than*? Listen again and repeat.

Unit 10 /θ/ (*think*) and /ð/ (*that*)

a ▶ **CD2 T11** Listen and repeat the words.

1 think   three   month   something   toothache
2 that   those   the   brother   sunbathing

b ▶ **CD2 T12** Listen and repeat the phrases. Underline *th* when the sound is /θ/. Circle *th* when the sound is /ð/.

1 Give me those things.
2 There's nothing in my mouth.
3 I think it's Thursday.

Unit 11 'll

a ▶ CD2 T16 Listen and check (✓) the sentence you hear.

1 a I ask the teacher. ☐
  b I'll ask the teacher. ☐
2 a They go to school early. ☐
  b They'll go to school early. ☐
3 a We have a lot of work to do. ☐
  b We'll have a lot of work to do. ☐
4 a I go to Boston by train. ☐
  b I'll go to Boston by train. ☐

Unit 12 /oʊ/ (go)

a ▶ CD2 T22 Listen and repeat the words.

show no homework clothes
boat snow

b ▶ CD2 T23 Listen to the sentences. Underline the words or syllables that have the /oʊ/ sound. Then listen again, check and repeat.

1 She was the only person who survived.
2 She walked slowly along the river.
3 The plane exploded.
4 When she woke up, she was alone.

Unit 13 *be going to*

▶ CD2 T29 *Going to* often sounds like *gonna* in spoken English. Listen and repeat these sentences.

1 Wendy is going to start a new business.
2 It's going to be sunny tomorrow!
3 Are they going to take up karate?
4 I'm going to be a pilot when I grow up.

Unit 14 Stress in conditional sentences

a ▶ CD2 T35 Listen to the sentences. Which words are stressed? Why? Underline the stressed words or syllables.

1 If it rains, I won't go to the beach.
2 We won't pass the test if we don't work hard.
3 I'll give him the card if I see him.
4 If you decide to come, I'll meet you at the restaurant.
5 She won't arrive on time if she misses the train.

b ▶ CD2 T35 Listen again and repeat.

Unit 15 Silent consonants

a ▶ CD2 T43 Listen and repeat the words. In each word below, there is a "silent" consonant that we don't pronounce. Underline the silent consonants.

1 honest 2 should 3 school
4 write 5 climb 6 know 7 two

b ▶ CD2 T44 Which consonants are silent in these words? Listen, check and repeat.

1 shouldn't 2 wrong 3 foreign
4 listen 5 island 6 hour

Unit 16 *have* and *has* in the present perfect

▶ CD3 T03 How are *have* and *has* pronounced? Listen and repeat.

A: *Have you ever driven a car?*
B: *Yes, I have.*

A: *Has she ever studied a foreign language?*
B: *Yes, she has.*

Speaking exercises: Student B

Unit 10, page 70, Exercise 14a

Student B: Ask Student A questions about their vacation to find out where they are going, how they are traveling and what kinds of activities they are going to do there.

Student B:

Destination: Tanzania

Dates: January 4 – January 25

Travel Arrangements: Fly to Julius Nyerere International Airport, Dar Es Salaam

Hotel: Holiday Inn, Dar Es Salaam

Trips: Safari in the Serengeti, trip to Zanzibar

Activities: Diving near Oyster Bay

Unit 12, page 84, Exercise 13

Student B: Look at your card. Answer Student A's questions. Then ask Student A questions in order to complete the information on the card.

Famous athlete	
Full name:	
Date of birth:	
Place of birth:	
Sport:	
First team:	
In 2004 _____	
In 2004, she also _____ .	
In 2006 and 2007, she _____ .	

Famous athlete

Full name: Kevin Maurice Garnett

Date of birth: May 19, 1976

Place of birth: Mauldin, South Carolina

Sport: basketball

Began playing when he was still in elementary school.

In 1995, he started playing for the Minnesota Timberwolves.

In 1999, he became a superstar.

In 2008, he won the NBA championship with the Boston Celtics.

Unit 14, page 93, Exercise 3

Student B: Look at the questions. Ask your questions and answer you partner's.

Student B

1 What will you do if you stay at home this weekend?

2 What will you study if you go to college?

3 What will you buy if you go shopping this weekend?

4 How will you feel if your parents ask you to do a lot of chores this evening?

5 Where will you travel if you go abroad on holiday this year?

6 Where will you go if you meet your friends tonight?

Unit 15, page 101, Exercise 3

Student B: Read the role card. Take turns listening to your partner's problem and give advice with *should* or *shouldn't*.

Student B

You love baseball, and you love your favorite baseball team. But you have a problem. You are going to your best friend's birthday party on Saturday. But now you know that your team has an important game on Saturday, too. You want to see the game, but you don't want to hurt your friend's feelings. Should you go to the game? Should you go to the party? Ask Student A.

Project 1

A poster about student life

1 Brainstorm

a You are going to make a poster and give a presentation about student life. Work in a group of four or five. In your group, decide on a topic you all want to work on. For example:

- school subjects
- school sports
- school clubs
- school rules
- free time activities
- volunteer opportunities for students
- jobs for students

b List as many ideas as you can for your topic. Discuss each idea and have one person write notes. For example, if you choose the topic "school clubs," you can write:

- Our school has 10 clubs: the photography club, the chess club, ...
- In the photography club, students learn to take pictures. In the chess club, ...
- The photography club meets on Wednesdays at 5:00. The chess club meets ...

2 Make the poster

a Find or draw pictures for your topic. For example, you can find pictures from your school's website, in magazines or on the Internet. If you can't find photos, you can draw your own pictures.

b Write short texts for your pictures. For example:

In the photography club, students learn to take pictures. The club meets on Wednesdays at 5:00. There are 20 students in the club.

c At the top of your poster, write a title for your topic. For example:

School Clubs

Arrange your pictures and texts below the title. If you have a computer to use, you can make a slideshow instead of a poster.

3 Presentation

Present your poster or slideshow to the other students in your class. Be ready to answer questions about it.

Project 2

A presentation about a well-known athlete

1 Brainstorm

a Look through Units 5–8 to find texts that give information about people. Quickly read through these texts again.

b Think of an athlete you want to find out about. Think about:

- recent sporting events you have seen on TV or read about.
- a person taking part in one of those events who impressed you.
- why this person impressed you.

c Work in a group and ask one student to take notes. Brainstorm ideas to decide who you will do your project on. What do you know about this person and what do you want to find out?

2 Research

With a partner or on your own, find out as much as possible about the person you chose. Use the Internet or look up information in books or magazines, in a library or at home.

Questions to think about:

- When was he/she born?
- What can you find out about his/her childhood?
- What sport does he/she do?
- What was his/her biggest success?
- Why was/is this person so successful?
- What kind of person is he/she?

3 Presentation

In your group, put together all the information you have. Decide how you will organize your presentation. For example:

- Start with a picture that you uncover piece by piece. Ask the class to guess who your presentation is going to be about.
- Take turns presenting the facts about the person.
- Finish your presentation with each member of the group saying what they admire most about the person.

Project 3
A class survey

1 Prepare the survey

a Work in small groups (three or four students). Choose one of the following topics:

- Learning languages
- Going on vacation
- Life in the future

b In your group, think of five questions that you can ask other students about your topic. For example:

> **Learning languages**
>
> How often do you get an opportunity to talk to someone in a foreign language?
>
> What do you like / not like about learning a foreign language?
>
> Would you like to learn more languages when you graduate?

c Make a questionnaire with your questions. For example:

> 1 How often do you talk or write to someone in a foreign language?
>
>   never / on vacation / once a month / more than once a month
>
> 2 Would you like to learn more languages when you graduate?　　　Yes/No
>
> 3 What do you like about learning a foreign language?
>
>   It's great to communicate with others in another language.　☐
>
>   It helps you understand another culture better.　☐
>
>   It's interesting to learn new words.　☐
>
>   It's great to understand songs in another language.　☐

Make sure that everyone in your group has a copy of the questionnaire.

d Use your questionnaire. Ask as many other students in your class as you can, and write down their answers.

2 Write about the results

a Go back to your group and put all of your answers together. For some questions, you can draw a chart.

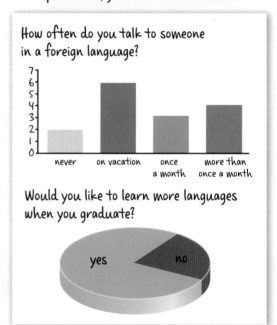

How often do you talk to someone in a foreign language?

Would you like to learn more languages when you graduate?

b Write a short report about the interviews.

c Arrange your sentences and charts on a poster under your topic heading. Add pictures if you want to.

3 Present your information

Use your poster to make a group presentation to the rest of the class.

Project 4

A talk about an event that happened this year

1 Listen

▶ CD3 T07 Listen to the beginning of three talks about memorable events that happened this year. What were the events?

2 Choose a topic

Spend some time thinking about the event that you will choose. Will you talk about an event that happened to you or an event that happened somewhere in the world? Will you talk about something sad, something happy or something funny?

3 Plan

a Think about these questions:

- When and where did the event take place?
- Is there any background information that you will need to explain the event?
- What happened?
- Why was it memorable? How did you feel about it at the time? How do you feel about it now?

b Make a list of important words you will want to use. If you aren't sure of some words, look them up in a dictionary or ask your teacher. Then use the words to help you write notes for your talk. Don't write everything down in complete sentences – just write important phrases that will help you remember what you want to say.

c Collect any information you need about your topic. If you can, find pictures, drawings or photographs that might help you to make your talk more interesting.

d Practice your talk quietly to yourself.

4 Give the talk

Work in a group of four or five. Each student gives his/her talk to the others in the group. Be prepared to answer questions at the end of your talk.

Irregular verbs

Base form	Simple past	Past participle
be	was/were	been
become	became	become
begin	began	begun
bite	bit	bitten
break	broke	broken
build	built	built
buy	bought	bought
can	could	could
catch	caught	caught
choose	chose	chosen
come	came	come
cut	cut	cut
do	did	done
drive	drove	driven
eat	ate	eaten
fall	fell	fallen
feel	felt	felt
find	found	found
fly	flew	flown
get	got	gotten
give	gave	given
go	went	gone
grow	grew	grown
have	had	had
hear	heard	heard
hit	hit	hit
hurt	hurt	hurt
keep	kept	kept
know	knew	known
leave	left	left
lose	lost	lost

Base form	Simple past	Past participle
make	made	made
meet	met	met
put	put	put
read	read	read
ride	rode	ridden
run	ran	run
say	said	said
see	saw	seen
sell	sold	sold
send	sent	sent
sit	sat	sat
sleep	slept	slept
speak	spoke	spoken
stand	stood	stood
swim	swam	swum
take	took	taken
teach	taught	taught
tell	told	told
think	thought	thought
throw	threw	thrown
understand	understood	understood
wake	woke	woken
win	won	won
write	wrote	written

Thanks and acknowledgments

The authors would like to thank a number of people whose support has proved invaluable during the planning, writing and production process of *American English in Mind*.

First of all we would like to thank the numerous teachers and students in many countries of the world who have used the first edition of *English in Mind*. Their enthusiasm for the course, and the detailed feedback and valuable suggestions we got from many of them were an important source of inspiration and guidance for us in developing the concept and in the creation of *American English in Mind*.

In particular, the authors and publishers would like to thank the following teachers who gave up their valuable time for classroom observations, interviews and focus groups:

Brazil
Warren Cragg (ASAP Idiomas); Angela Pinheiro da Cruz (Colégio São Bento; Carpe Diem); Ana Paula Vedovato Maestrello (Colégio Beatíssima Virgem Maria); Natália Mantovanelli Fontana (Lord's Idiomas); Renata Condi de Souza (Colégio Rio Branco, Higienópolis Branch); Alexandra Arruda Cardoso de Almeida (Colégio Guilherme Dumont Villares / Colégio Emilie de Villeneuve); Gisele Siqueira (Speak Up); Ana Karina Giusti Mantovani (Idéia Escolas de Línguas); Maria Virgínia G. B. de Lebron (UFTM / private lessons); Marina Piccinato (Speak Up); Patrícia Nero (Cultura Inglesa / Vila Mariana); Graziela Barroso (Associação Alumni); Francisco Carlos Peinado (Wording); Maria Lúcia Sciamarelli (Colégio Divina Providencia / Jundiaí); Deborah Hallal Jorge (Nice Time Language Center); Lilian Itzicovitch Leventhal (Colégio I. L. Peretz); Dulcinéia Ferreira (One Way Línguas); and Priscila Prieto and Carolina Cruz Marques (Seven Idiomas).

Colombia
Luz Amparo Chacón (Gimnasio Los Monjes); Mayra Barrera; Diana de la Pava (Colegio de la Presentación Las Ferias); Edgar Ardila (Col. Mayor José Celestino Mutis); Sandra Cavanzo B. (Liceo Campo David); Claudia Susana Contreras and Luz Marína Zuluaga (Colegio Anglo Americano); Celina Roldán and Angel Torres (Liceo Cervantes del Norte); Nelson Navarro; Maritza Ruiz Martín; Francisco Mejía, and Adriana Villalba (Colegio Calasanz).

Ecuador
Paul Viteri (Colegio Andino, Quito); William E. Yugsan (Golden Gate Academy – Quito); Irene Costales (Unidad Educativa Cardinal Spellman Femenino); Vinicio Sanchez and Sandra Milena Rodríguez (Colegio Santo Domingo de Guzmán); Sandra Rigazio and María Elena Moncayo (Unidad Educativa Tomás Moro, Quito); Jenny Alexandra Jara Recalde and Estanislao Javier Pauta (COTAC, Quito); Verónica Landázuri and Marisela Madrid (Unidad Educativa "San Francisco de Sales"); Oswaldo Gonzalez and Monica Tamayo (Angel Polibio Chaves School, Quito); Rosario Llerena and Tania Abad (Isaac Newton, Quito); María Fernanda Mármol Mazzini and Luis Armijos (Unidad Educativa Letort, Quito); and Diego Bastidas and Gonzalo Estrella (Colegio Gonzaga, Quito).

Mexico
Connie Alvarez (Colegio Makarenko); Julieta Zelinski (Colegio Williams); Patricia Avila (Liceo Ibero Mexicano); Patricia Cervantes de Brofft (Colegio Frances del Pedregal); Alicia Sotelo (Colegio Simon Bolivar); Patricia Lopez (Instituto Mexico, A.C.); Maria Eugenia Fernandez Castro (Instituto Oriente Arboledas); Lilian Ariadne Lozano Bustos (Universidad Tecmilenio); Maria del Consuelo Contreras Estrada (Liceo Albert Einstein); Alfonso Rene Pelayo Garcia (Colegio Tomas Alva Edison); Ana Pilar Gonzalez (Instituto Felix de Jesus Rougier); and Blanca Kreutter (Instituto Simon Bolivar).

Our heartfelt thanks go to the *American English in Mind* team for their cooperative spirit, their many excellent suggestions and their dedication, which have been characteristic of the entire editorial process: Paul Phillips, Amy E. Hawley, Kelley Perrella, Eric Zuarino, Pam Harris, Kate Powers, Brigit Dermott, Kate Spencer, Heather McCarron, Keaton Babb, Roderick Gammon, Hugo Loyola, Howard Siegelman, Colleen Schumacher, Margaret Brooks, Kathryn O'Dell, Genevieve Kocienda, Lisa Hutchins, and Lynne Robertson.

We would also like to thank the teams of educational consultants, representatives and managers working for Cambridge University Press in various countries around the world. Space does not allow us to mention them all by name here, but we are extremely grateful for their support and their commitment.

In Student's Book 2, thanks go to David Crystal for the interview in Unit 9, and to Jon Turner for giving us the idea of using the story of Ulises de la Cruz in Unit 15.

Thanks to the team at Pentacor Book Design for giving the book its design; the staff at Full House Productions for the audio recordings; and Lightning Pictures and Mannic Media for the video.

Last but not least, we would like to thank our partners, Mares and Adriana, for their support.

The publishers are grateful to the following illustrators:
Dylan Gibson, Graham Kennedy, Kel Dyson (Bright), David Shephard (Bright), Mark Watkinson (Illustration), Laura Martinez (Sylvie Poggio), Paul McCaffrey (Sylvie Poggio), Richard Williams (Eastwing).

The publishers are grateful to the following for permission to reproduce photographic material:
Alamy/©Art Kowalsky p 64 (bl),), /©Associated Sports Photography p 104 (tr), /©ImagesEurope p 34 (tl), /©David Lyons p 46 (G), /©Photos 12 p 42, /©Jochen Tack p 46 (L), /©WorldFoto p 44 (tl), /©David Young-Wolffp 48 (tl); ©Biblioteca Universitaria di Bologna p 58 (t); Aquarius Collection/Columbia TriStar p 30 (br); Cache Agency/©Chuck Krall p 90 (l); China Pictorial Supplement, Courtesy of the ITTF; Corbis p 46 (A, J), /©Peter Beck p 95 (tl), /©Bettmann p 73 (cl), /©Kevin Dodge p 59 (l), /©John Harper p 112 (New York), /©Jason Hawkes p 34 (ct), /©Steve Hix/Somos Images p 46 (B), /©Rainer Jensen/dpa p 95 (br), /©Michael A. Keller p 28 (l), /©James Marshall p 50, /©Jacques Pavlovsky/Sygma p 90(r), /©Qi Heng/Xinhua Press p 117, /©Reuters pp 66 (b),108, /©Andersen Ross/ Blend Images p 59 (r), /©Bjorn Sigurdson/epa p 44 (tr), /©Carlos Silva/Reuters p 33 (tr), /©Zave Smith p 46 (H), /©Pauline St. Denis p 28 (r), /©Thinkstock p 64 (br);© David Crystal p 60 (t); Education Photos/John Walmsley p 46 (D, F); Getty Images/AFP p 86 (b), /AFP/Gent Shkullaku p 106 (bl), /Dorling Kindersley/Alex Robinson p 33 (bl), /Hulton Archive p 73 (tl), /Hulton Archive/Archive Holdings Inc. p 73 (tcl), /Hulton Collection p 73 (b), /Sean Justice p 121, /David McNew p 30 (tr, br), /National Archives p 34 (cr), /Photographer's Choice/ Luis Veiga p 35 (bl), /Photonica/Colin Gray p 62 (br), /Stock4B/Arne Pastoor p 22 (tr), / Matthew Stockman p 44 (bl), /Stone/David Ball p 34 (br), /Stone/Michael Heinsen p 46 (E), /Stone/Ryan McVay p 112 (concert), /Taxi/Michael Blann p 48 (bl), /Taxi/Frank Herholdt p 63, /Taxi/Jeff Sherman p 95 (tr), /WireImage/ Jeff Vespa p 44 (br); ©GUINNESS WORLD RECORDS p 102 (tl); ©Masterfile p 46 (l); /age fotostock/Javier Larrea p 46 (K), /age fotostock/ Jack Milchanowski p 112 (snake), /Fresh Food Images/Dominic Dibbs p 56 (b), /Fresh Food Images/ Rob Greig/Time Out p 56 (tr), /Robert Harding Travel/Sergio Pitamitz p 34 (tr), /Japan Travel Bureau/JTB Photo pp 66 (t), 104 (tl), /View Pictures/Grant Smith p 56 (tl), Press Association Images/AP p 79, /AP/Frank Franklin II p 92, / AP/Seth Wenig p 86 (t), /Everett Collection p 73 (c), /Laurence Kiely p 73 (tcr), /Shout p 48 (tr), /Sipa Press p 84, /Shutterstock Images p 95 (c), /Els Jooren p 112 (paraglider), /Andrei Merkulov p 46 (C), /Matsonashvili Mikhail p 112 (Maldives), /Maxim Petrichuk p 112 (helicopter), /photogl p 112 (mountain top), / RTimages p 112 (trophy), /Ljupco Smokovski p 95 (bl), /Zuzule p 112 (horse); Still Pictures/©Ron Giling p 22; The Thayer Collection p 35 (tr). Shutterstock/©Dmitriy Shironosov p 2 (t), Shutterstock/©Debra James p 5 (br), Shutterstock/©Jerry Horbert p 10 (theater), istockphoto.com/©Karin Lau p 10 (train), Shutterstock/©Monkey Business Images p 10 (bookshop), Shutterstock/©dwphotos p 10 (dancing), Shutterstock/©Karkas p 10 (shoe store), Shutterstock/©iofoto p 10 (cafe), Shutterstock/©R. Michael Ballard p 10 (post office), Shutterstock/©Christina Richards p 10 (store), Shutterstock/©Noam Armonn p 18 (swimmer), Shutterstock/©Yuri Arcurs p 18 (mp3), Shutterstock/©Yuri Arcurs p 18 (disco), Shutterstock/©AVAVA p 18 (video game), Getty Images/Taxi/©Erik Dreyer p 18 (movie tickets), Shutterstock/©Ivanova Inga p 18 (reading), Shutterstock/©Val Thoermer p 18 (jogging), Shutterstock/©Matt Antonino p 18 (painting), Shutterstock/©Roxana Gonzalez p 18 (guitar), Ellen McKnight p 20 (t), Alamy/©Kumar Sriskandan p 21 (cl), Alamy/©Aflo Foto Agency p 21 (tl), Shutterstock/©Bill Lawson p 25 (tl), Shutterstock/©Yuri Arcurs p 25 (tc), Shutterstock/©Monkey Business Images p 25 (tr), Shutterstock/©Alexey Avdeev p 25 (cl), Shutterstock/©Jiri Miklo p 25 (cr), Shutterstock/©Monkey Business Images p 25 (bc&br), Shutterstock/©fotum p 45 (tl), istockphoto.com/©Ariel Duhon p 45 (tr), Shutterstock/©Anyka p 45 (cl), istockphoto.com/©Izabela Habur p 45 (cr), Shutterstock/©liseykina p 45 (bl), Shutterstock/©AVAVA p 45 (br), Getty Images for NASCAR/©Geoff Burke p 47 (r&l), istockphoto.com/©YinYang p 48 (br), Alamy/©Jaak Nilson p 49 (bl), Shutterstock/©Sergey Peterman p 52 (tl), Shutterstock/©Olga Lyubkina p 52 (tr), Shutterstock/©Schmid Christophe p 52 (cl), Shutterstock/©Mathias Wilson p 52 (cr), Shutterstock/©Martin Allinger p 52 (bl), Shutterstock/©Phil Date p 52 (br), istockphoto.com/©Catherine Yeulet p 62 (t), istockphoto. com/©Rafal Belzowski p 64 (tr), Alamy/©Michael Patrick O'Neill p 64 (cl), Shutterstock/©David P. Lewis p 64 (cr), Alamy/©Jason Bazzano p 64 (bl), Alamy/©NASA Images p 73 (rocket), istockphoto.com/©Spiderstock p 73 (tc), Shutterstock/©Four Oaks p 74 (l), istockphoto.com/©Julie de Leseleuc p 76 (l), istockphoto.com/©Laurent davoust p 76 (cl), Getty Images/©SSPL p 76 (cr), Shutterstock/©ifong p 76 (r), AP Photo/©Dolores Ochoa R. p 105 (tc), Sun Media/London Free Press/©Derek Ruttan p 106 (bc), Getty Images/WireImage for PMK/© HBH/©G. Gershoff p 106 (br), Shutterstock/©Victor Newman p 109 (yawn), Alamy/©brt PHOTO p 112 (cr), Getty Images/©Purestock p 118 (tl), istockphoto.com/©matt mathews p 118 (tc), Alamy/©Catchlight Visual Services p 118 (tr), Getty Images/Photographer's Choice/©Andy Sacks p 118 (b)

The publishers are grateful to the following for their assistance with commissioned photographs: Mannic Media

DVD-ROM Instructions

American English in Mind can be run directly from the DVD-ROM and does not require installation. However, you can also install *American English in Mind* and run it from your hard drive. This will make the DVD-ROM run more quickly.

Start the DVD-ROM

Windows PC
- Insert the *American English in Mind* DVD-ROM into your DVD-ROM drive.
- If Autorun is enabled, the DVD-ROM will start automatically.
- If Autorun is not enabled, open **My Computer** and then **D:** (where D is the letter of your DVD-ROM drive). Then double click on the *American English in Mind* icon.

Mac OS X
- Insert the *American English in Mind* DVD-ROM into your DVD-ROM drive.
- Double-click on the DVD-ROM icon on your desktop to open it.
- Double-click on the *American English in Mind* Mac OS X icon.

Install the DVD-ROM to your hard drive (recommended)

Windows PC
- Go to **My Computer** and then **D:** (where D is the letter of your DVD-ROM drive).
- Right-click on *Explore*.
- Double-click on *Install American English in Mind to hard drive*.
- Follow the installation instructions on your screen.

Mac OS X
- Double-click on the DVD-ROM icon on your desktop to open it.
- Create a folder on your computer.
- Copy the content of the DVD-ROM into this folder.
- Double-click on the *American English in Mind* Mac OS X icon.

Listen and practice on your CD player
You can listen to and practice language from the Student's Book Pronunciation, Culture in Mind and Photostory activities. You can also listen to and practice the Workbook Pronunciation and Listening activities.

What's on the DVD-ROM?
- **Interactive practice activities**
  Extra practice of Grammar, Vocabulary, English Pronunciation, Reading and Writing. Click on a set of unit numbers (1–2 through 15–16) at the top of the screen. Then choose an activity and click on it to start.
- **Word list**
  Pronunciation and definitions. Click on *Word list* on the left side of the screen. Then choose a word to hear its pronunciation. You can also add your own notes.
- **Self-test**
  Click on *Self-test*, and choose a set of unit numbers (1–2 through 15–16) on the left side of the screen. You can also test yourself on multiple sets of units.
- **Game**
  This is extra practice of Grammar and Vocabulary. Click on the game controller icon at the top of the screen. Click on a set of unit numbers (1–2 through 15–16), and choose a character. Click on start to begin the game. You can also choose all the units.

System Requirements
- 512MB of RAM (1GB recommended for video)
- 1GB free hard disk space (if installing to hard disk)
- 800 x 600 resolution or higher
- speakers or headphones
- a microphone if you wish to record yourself speaking

For PC
- Windows XP, Vista or 7

For Mac
- Mac OSX 10.4 or 10.5
- 1.2 GHz G4 processor or higher

Support
If you experience difficulties with this DVD-ROM, please visit: http://www.cambridge.org/elt/multimedia/help

---

Song/Text Acknowledgments
"You've Got a Friend in Me" on p. 39 WORDS AND MUSIC BY RANDY NEWMAN
(C) WALT DISNEY MUSIC (USA) CO (ASCAP) ALL RIGHTS ADMINISTERED BY WARNER/CHAPPELL ARTEMIS MUSIC LTD. You've Got a Friend in Me from Walt Disney's Toy Story Music and Lyrics by Randy Newman. ©1995 Walt Disney Music Company. All rights reserved. Used by permission.
Reprinted by permission of Hal Leonard Corporation
Sound a-like recording by Marathon Media International. Copyright © Marathon Media International;

"When I'm 64" on p. 75 © 1967 (Renewed 1995) Sony / ATV Tunes LLC. All rights administered by Sony / ATV Music Publishing, 8 Music Square West, Nashville, TN 37203. All rights reserved. Used by permission. Sound a-like recording by Marathon Media International. Copyright © Marathon Media International;

"Wonderful World, Beautiful People" on p. 91 Words and Music by Jimmy Cliff Copyright © 1969 ISLAND MUSIC LTD. Copyright renewed All Rights for the United States and Canada Administered by Universal – Songs of Polygram International, Inc. All rights reserved. Used by permission.
Reprinted by permission of Hal Leonard Corporation
Words & Music by Jimmy Cliff © Copyright 1969 Island Music Limited. Universal/Island Music Limited. Used by permission of Music Sales Limited. All Rights Reserved. International Copyright Secured. Bell Voice Recordings for the sound a-like recording;

For the adapted article on p. 92 "Man is Rescued by Stranger on Subway Tracks" from the New York Times, N.Y. Region Section 1/3/2007 The New York Times All rights reserved. Used by permission and protection by the Copyright Laws of the United States. The printing, copying, redistribution, or retransmission of the Material without express written permission is prohibited.